THE VISIONS OF RON HERRON

Architectural Monographs No 38

THE VISIONS OF RON HERRON

REYNER BANHAM

A.D. ACADEMY EDITIONS

TRIBUTE TO REYNER BANHAM

I am proud and honoured that the commentaries in this book were written by Peter Reyner Banham, architectural historian, journalist, critic, lecturer, teacher, theorist – and my friend for almost twenty-five years. He was a man whose comments, criticism and encouragement I always sought and valued.

Peter produced the outline for the essays in May 1987. In September that year, during a brief visit to London from his Santa Cruz home, he spent five or six days in my Clerkenwell studio looking through my notebooks, reminding himself of the early work, catching up on the recent drawings, and scanning projects on the computer screen. After that he put the first draft into the studio Apple Mac. He made the second draft in Santa Cruz just before he took ill. And, ever professional, he made the final edit in the Royal Free Hospital, London, in February 1988. Sadly, Peter Banham died on the 19th of March 1988.

When I first met Peter he was already a major figure on the architectural scene, well known for his book, *Theory and Design in the First Machine Age*, his articles in *The Architectural Review* and *The Architects' Journal*, the ideas he explored in his *New Statesman* and *New Society* pieces, and his involvement with the Independent Group and their exhibition, 'This is Tomorrow', at the Whitechapel Art Gallery in 1956. All of us in the Archigram Group were eager to meet Peter and when we did, we found someone we could relate to, whose inquiries into popular culture and the reality of expendability paralleled and extended our own investigations into commercial imagery, current technology, 'pop' and expendable architecture. Peter, in 1964, took the 'Zoom' issue of *Archigram* magazine to the US and moved Archigram into the international architectural scene.

Memories of conversations come flooding back – conversations about Los Angeles, about megastructures, robotics, the space programme, science fiction, movies, pop art, technology in architecture and the delights of the Apple Macintosh. Memories of meetings. A picnic of take-away fried chicken on Santa Monica beach, Thanksgiving Day, 1969. Brunch at the Gamble House, LA, where Peter lived while he was teaching at the University of Southern California. Evenings at the Cooks' and Banhams' in Aberdare Gardens in the 1960s and early 1970s. Bumping into the Banhams – Mary, Ben, Debbie and Peter – at the drag races at Santa Pod and the delight of strolling through the pits with a running commentary from Peter and Ben on the technical merits of the various dragsters and a potted history of the vehicles, drivers, teams and paint jobs. Showing Peter, in 1987, the 'Studio Strip' video incorporating computer animation, real video and studio tricks, and his understanding of and delight in what we were attempting to simulate. These are but a few personal memories of a great and generous man who, for my generation, helped break the boundaries of art and architecture. He is greatly missed.

Ron Herron

The commentaries by Reyner Banham are accompanied by Ron Herron's own project descriptions (distinguished by bold type). While the architect says that he 'enjoys drawing to illustrate his ideas rather than writing about them', these descriptions communicate directly his own perspective on the work, setting out in an evocative, frank manner the thoughts behind the projects, their evolution, and what it is about them that fascinates or delights him.

Cover: **STUDIO STRIP, 1986**
Frontis: **IMAGINATION, 1988**

The photographs used in this publication have been provided by Imagination Limited, for its headquarters in Store Street, London WC1, and by the Workshop for Architecture and Urbanism, and the Urban Factory for the three projects in Japan. The photograph of the Instant City Airship on page 43 was taken by Christian Wachter. Photographic reproduction of the drawings from the sketchbooks and many of the other drawings by Catherine and Dennis Crompton.

Architectural Monographs No 38
First published in Great Britain in 1994 by

ACADEMY EDITIONS
An imprint of Academy Group Ltd
42 Leinster Gardens London W2 3AN
Member of VCH Publishing Group

House Editor: Maggie Toy
Art Editor: Andrea Bettella

Edited and designed by Dennis Crompton

ISBN 1 85490 268 7

Copyright © 1994 Text: Banham Estate
© This edition: Academy Group Ltd

The moral right of the author has been asserted

Distributed to the trade in the United States of America by
ST MARTIN'S PRESS
175 Fifth Avenue, New York, NY 10010

Printed and bound in Singapore

CONTENTS

OUTLINES OF REAL ILLUSIONS

AT FIRST SIGHT, the world of Ron Herron's drawings looks suspiciously like a theme park; cardboard public facades fronting mysterious zones filled with scaffolding and unexpected machinery clearly intended for the management of illusions. Yet these are not movie sets or *scenografie*; the mysteries manufactured behind the facades are no less important or consequential than the assertions made by their public elevations. Conventional outward show and radical interior fantasy are here created equal – and the ghostly chuckle you may hear in the historical background could, just, be Inigo Jones, who long ago laid down the ground-rules for the Great British Architectural Illusion: '*Outwardly every wyse man carrieth a Groviti in Publick Places, yet inwardly hath his imaginacy set on fire and sumtimes licenciously flying out, as nature hirself doeth often times stravagantly. . . .*'

BANQUET SET.

'Queens Rt'
Windsor
14·7·93.

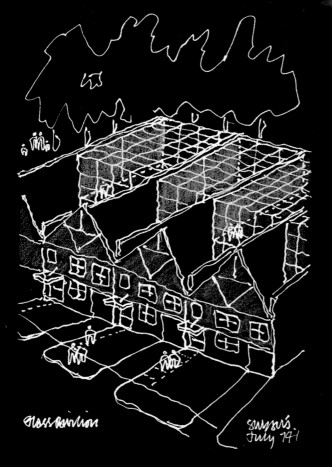

But then, again, the Herron world can also look more like dispensing machines or music-centres sitting unattended, snug and self-contained, in Arcadian glades, offering to transform a waste place into a Garden of unmistakably Earthly Delights. Or it can offer what appear to be space-vehicles, or historic dirigibles, dangling complex arrays of audio-visual equipment mockingly above ancient cities and Victorian suburbs, leaving what stands upon the ground transformed in meaning and use, yet unchanged in physical fabric, just as it can threaten to invade the interiors of existing structures and leave them utterly transmogrified, without disturbing a single brick or ancestral joist.

And first impressions do not utterly deceive; what is projected here is a very strange world indeed, where software inspires hardware to re-jig our given built-ware – a world made more disturbing for being only about a half-frame ahead of the current 'reality' which will come up on the screen, with no assistance from architects, after the next batch of commercials. Ron Herron has already been around long enough to see the allegedly impractical projects in his early sketches come true in the hands of other architects, and occasionally his own. However visionary, his drawings remain persuasive to so-called practical men, and the highly finished ones in particular contain (or appear to contain) plausible compónents and details and clip-on equipment for making it all happen, for making illusion realisably real. The drawn hardware may be no more than allegories, as it were, of real-world and real-time stuff, but it is rarely a long jump from the allegory to the actual hardware that will soon be on-line to do the job.

the ic blimp~ here

If one looks at his sketchbooks, however, rather than the block-busting presentation drawings, one can see that there may be a very good reason why there should be this sense of being less than a frame-scan away from practicality: at the level of his first-approximation sketches, the proposed structures and installations rarely seem to imply anything more than conventional current technologies of equipment and construction, bricolated together with off-the-shelf componentry – though not always from the world of regular architecture. And that too should come as no great surprise, since Herron's whole output is somewhat at variance with the world of regular architecture.

Paradoxically though, there can be no nonsense about him *not* being an architect. He is not a structural nor a systems engineer, in spite of his knowledge of both areas; he is not a computer whizz, nor even a hacker, though few living architects are quite so computer-friendly. He is in himself, and in his generation, entirely at home in the world of current technology, yet always and entirely an architect. He knows exactly what he is after when he goes round invading the professional turfs of adjacent specialisations (or even remote ones), but when he returns from these forays of design-piracy he does not appear bent over and burdened down, as were the Machine Aesthetes of the 1920s, with the weight and importance of the loot he has acquired. He still occupies his usual professional posture.

He never ceases to think and design like an architect, so that if his projects appear strange, they are no more than strange, rather than alien or threatening, to other architects, and the excitement that he derives from these forays is communicable to other architects by purely architectural means – or drawings, as they are more usually called.

The pleasures of the chase, the swagger of the returning explorer, are there even in the finished renderings, but you catch them raw and unmediated in the notebooks in which Ron Herron accumulates and refines his architectural concepts, or occasionally records visual goodies that come his way. The processes by which forms and ideas are burglarised from other fields are manifest there, but what is striking is that the means of acquisition themselves, the techniques of capture and domestication for architectural purposes, are entirely conventional, not to say traditional – a Pentel R50 ballpen, Magic Markers, all that kind of familiar stuff. Only a little material is collaged in as found; the historic method of architectural recording – *disegno, dessin, tekening, zeichnung,* drawing – is employed, and even his electronic outputs are computer graphics, right?

Trailer.
HERRON NOV 66'

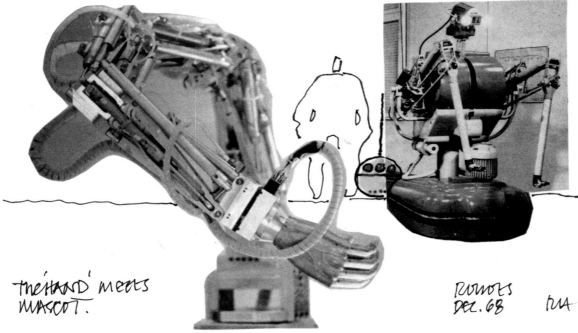

the 'HAND' meets MASCOT.

ROBOTS DEC. 68

MANZAK
DEC 1969 L.A.

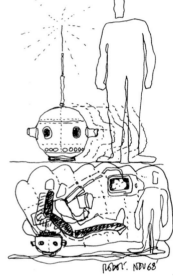

ROBOTS

Robots have cropped up in my work for many years. I am fascinated with the idea of the mechanical being, the servant-like object. 'Manzak' was one of the early versions of this; a tiny sort of puppy dog that would follow you around and be your companion. Like a motor car, it came with many optional extras, such as voice command, or the ability to open up and make an enclosed personal space, or turn into an audio-visual seat. It was a friendly little object that respected Asimov's five laws of robotics.

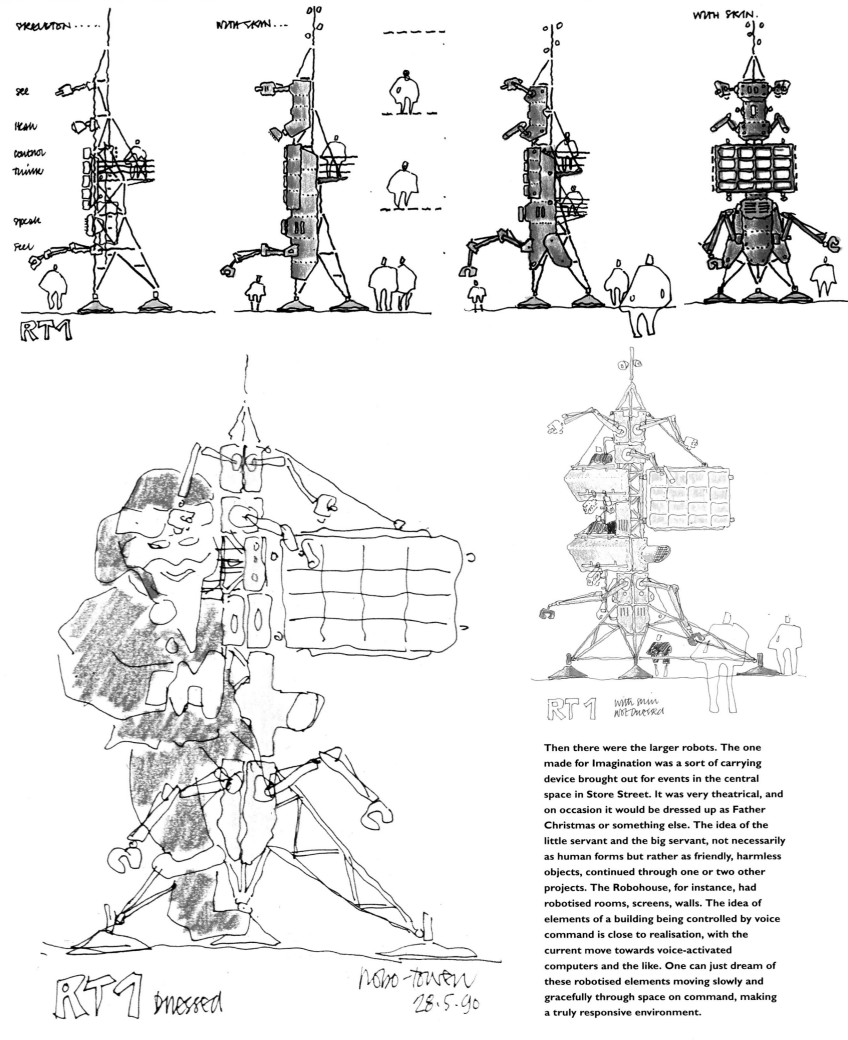

RT1

RT1 dressed

robo-tower
28.5.90

RT1 with skin not dressed

Then there were the larger robots. The one made for Imagination was a sort of carrying device brought out for events in the central space in Store Street. It was very theatrical, and on occasion it would be dressed up as Father Christmas or something else. The idea of the little servant and the big servant, not necessarily as human forms but rather as friendly, harmless objects, continued through one or two other projects. The Robohouse, for instance, had robotised rooms, screens, walls. The idea of elements of a building being controlled by voice command is close to realisation, with the current move towards voice-activated computers and the like. One can just dream of these robotised elements moving slowly and gracefully through space on command, making a truly responsive environment.

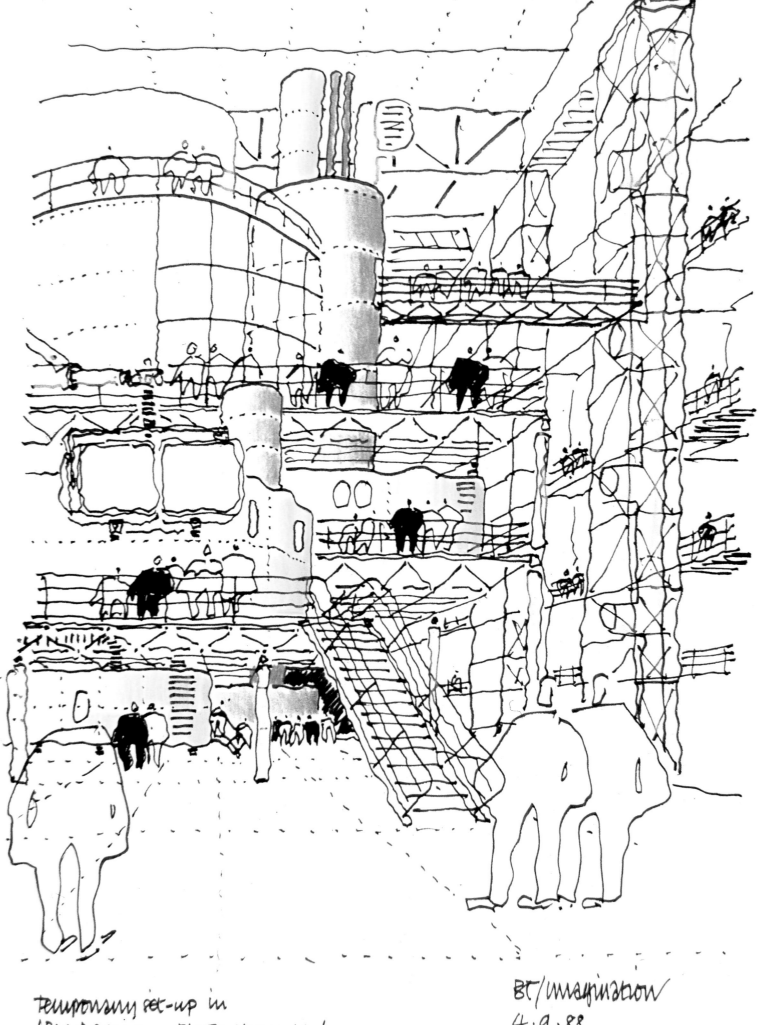

Temporary set-up in
'Big' space. - Floor mounted.

BT/Imagination
4.9.88

OUTLINES OF REAL ILLUSIONS

The point is important; what Ron Herron offers is architecture still, not product design (even when he designs a product) nor print-layout (even when he lays out print). The trained eye that can recognise the presence of architecture will also recognise the trained hand that cannot help making architecture. Now, that phrase 'making architecture' is, in the sense employed here, almost the copyright of Renzo Piano, an architect to whom Ron Herron is in some ways very close, though neither of them may have noticed it yet. The difference between them – which is crucial – is that Piano's oeuvre is mostly built, whereas Ron Herron's vision is still largely on paper. The similarity – which is even more crucial – is that both seem equally obsessed with making sense, straightforward architectural sense, of the cornucopia of materials and methods that has been spilled across architects' drafting-boards by 'modern technology' (as we used to call it in the innocent beginnings of High-Tech).

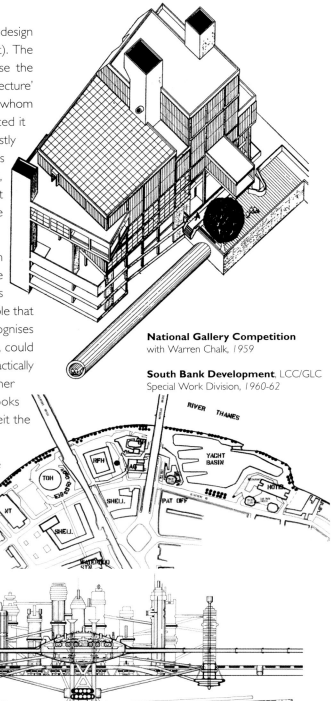

National Gallery Competition
with Warren Chalk, 1959

South Bank Development, LCC/GLC
Special Work Division, 1960-62

Piano's architecture is proverbially made *pezzo a pezzo*, piece by piece, and in each piece one can recognise the craftsmanly thinking that has gone into making it the right piece to make architecture, into turning the materials and technologies involved into components which, if assembled in the right order, make an ensemble that is as much architecture as were the pieces. And in Ron Herron's visions one recognises the draftsmanly creativity that has gone into hypothesising pieces which, if made, could be assembled in the right order to make architecture. But whereas in Piano's case practically every piece is a 'special', a total invention, the case with Herron is apt to be the other way around; that he has hypothesised a new architectural use for what looks unsettlingly like a commonplace component that is already in the catalogue (albeit the catalogue of some quite different human enterprise, as often as not).

In both cases, however, the objective seems to be the same, and it is the same obsessive objective that has been the power behind modern architecture since it became modern: to transmute the stuff of technology into the matter of architecture. Maybe that has been the power behind all architecture ever since it began, but for most of the three thousand-odd years that the noble art has been around, that transmutation had been done so long ago, and was so immemorially enshrined in the inherited practices of carpentry, brickwork and masonry that it took no conscious effort on any individual architect's part, and the conventions of draftsmanship could operate unquestioned as the means of indicating the artifice required to make architecture out of those comfortably conventional technologies.

City Interchange with Warren Chalk, 1963

But the iron-masters of the 18th century disinherited architects from those cosy old traditions, and after them came the steel-masters and the cement-masters and the glass-masters and the plastic-masters and the light-masters and the air-masters and the power-masters and the system-masters, all of whom have increased the distance that separates the business of making better buildings from the traditional art of making architecture.

Narrowing that gap to the point where it is once more possible to make architecture has been the substance of the patient search of Le Corbusier and the disciplined classicism of Mies van der Rohe and the mystical intuitions of Louis Kahn and the structural heroics of Buckminster Fuller… and the draftsmanly visions of Archigram, of whom Ron Herron is a conspicuous survivor. And, after Archigram (as they themselves would mostly admit) came Rogers, Foster and the whole 'High-Tech' tendency, with its fabricatory ingenuities, which are often as obsessive as Archigram drawings. That gap is not to be narrowed by dressing up

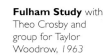

Fulham Study with Theo Crosby and group for Taylor Woodrow, 1963

Bridge, **Natural History Museum**, 1992

IN THE PUBLIC AREAS OF THE INFORMATION PLAZA BOGART MOVIES PLAY. A CITY BLOCK AWAY A MULTI-USER ADVENTURE GAME IS PLAYED OUT BY TEAMS FROM ALL OVER THE CITY

IN THE LOCAL INFORMATION PLAZA A LAW PROGRAMME GOES ON, STUDENTS INTERACTING WITH THE SYSTEM IN A LIVE REPLAY FROM THE SYSTEM'S COURT REPORTING DATA BANK

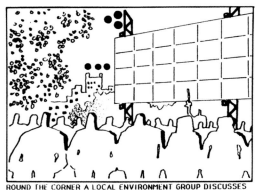

ROUND THE CORNER A LOCAL ENVIRONMENT GROUP DISCUSSES STRATEGY, AIDED BY THE INFORMATION SYSTEM, IMMEDIATE PEOPLE INPUT, INSTANT LOCAL DEMOCRACY

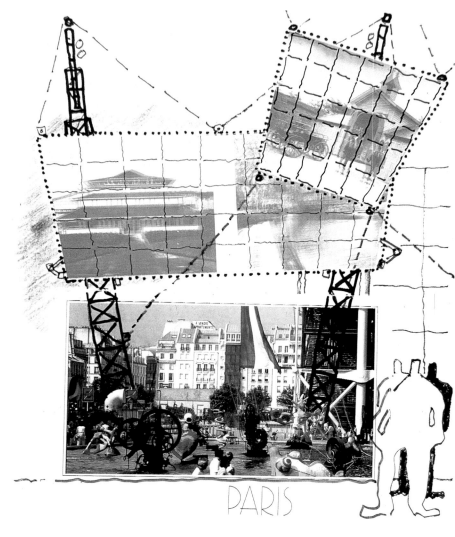

PARIS

Kawasaki competition with Dennis Crompton, 1986

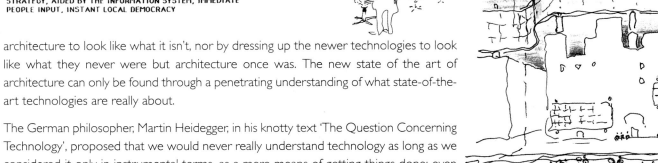

architecture to look like what it isn't, nor by dressing up the newer technologies to look like what they never were but architecture once was. The new state of the art of architecture can only be found through a penetrating understanding of what state-of-the-art technologies are really about.

The German philosopher, Martin Heidegger, in his knotty text 'The Question Concerning Technology', proposed that we would never really understand technology as long as we considered it only in instrumental terms, as a mere means of getting things done; even 'the correct instrumental definition of technology still does not show us technology's essence'. Several knotted pages later he almost blows the whole proposition by announcing that 'The essence of technology is in a lofty sense ambiguous. [Thanks a bunch, Martin!] Such ambiguity points to the mystery of all revealing, i.e., of truth.'

From here on, Heidegger's avowed destination is to discover the essence of Art, Life, and all those traditional lofty abstractions, rather than the essences of commonplace technologies. But let us hold on to that idea of revelation and truth. All the breakthroughs

MARSHAM STREET

I proposed that the Department of the Environment site in Marsham Street should be cleared and turned into an electronic forum for unpartisan political debate – a place for people to question political opinions and decisions, drawing on constantly updated information. Live video images would set up an electronic conversation activated by touch screens, keyboards and voice. Also on site would be a large enclosure containing bookable meeting rooms, a flexible, responsive meeting space, a public restaurant, an outlet for HMSO printing and communication services, and public access television studios. The plaza would be connected with other forums located throughout the country, creating an interactive parliament in the true sense of the word.

towards an architecture of technology have been, in a literal sense, revelations – of how to make architecture, that pure creation of the human spirit, out of concrete, or steel, or glass, or whatever. And each revelation that has comprehended or uncovered an essence – the Villa Savoye, the Farnsworth House, just as much as the Pantheon or La Sainte Chapelle – has been a truth out of which architects can make architecture.

Not all such revelations have to be buildings. They could be a paragraph from Ruskin's *Stones of Venice*, or Geoffrey Scott's *Architecture of Humanism*, or even Asimov's *Caves of Steel*. But architects being the visual, graphics-besotted creatures they are, the revelations are more likely to be engraved plates in the works of Viollet-le-Duc, or the patent application drawing that revealed the essence of Le Corbusier's Maison Dom-ino, the space-cathedral sketches of Bruno Taut or the renderings of imaginary skyscrapers by Hugh Ferris, the Fun Palace drawings of Cedric Price, the coloured collages of Archigram's Peter Cook … or Ron Herron's Walking City drawing, a long-legged revelation stalking the surface of the globe, a truth or illusion in search of a site on which to settle and become real.

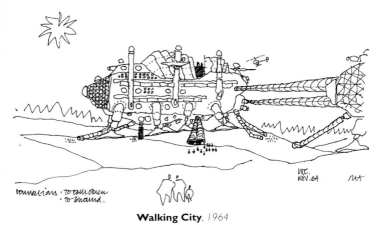

Walking City, 1964

La Défense competition with Warren Chalk, 1983

For the power of this revelation, what gives it the illusion of truth, is that it has the plausibility of a fully worked out concept. Not the plausibility of a finished design, because the slightest of Ron Herron's sketches often show that same plausibility: they too exude the air of being the work of an architect who knows what he is about, and has got it all straight in his head, even if some ultimate details of form or connection remain to be worked out. Closely examined, the Walking City drawing clearly awaits the resolution of many such details, since there is no way it could actually operate in physical, instrumental fact as the drawing now stands. Yet it delivers a powerful illusion of reality, a kind of mirror-image or counter-vision to the detailed plausibility of the gismology behind the facades of his Suburban Sets that really looks as if it could make illusion real.

But then, the work of the architect as he bends over the paper, pencil in hand, is all illusion. He produces simulacra of reality, diagrams which, by some form of sympathetic magic, are supposed to cause real buildings to happen out in the instrumental world. We all know that it is not sympathetic magic but a vast and frequently fallible industrial complex that will turn the illusory vision into real construction but, for architects, the moment of magic, the revelation of truth, is when the pencil marks the paper, and the process of making architecture begins.

TRACES OF HISTORY (*opposite*)
The Traces of History project grew out of an interest in trying to combine new with old – a common theme throughout the history of architecture. It began with a visit about 20 years ago to the Acropolis, when I saw the Erechtheum and Parthenon partly wrapped in scaffolding. I had the idea of making a kind of protective showcase for the cultural object. The wrapping protects the historical piece but at the same time changes continually. It becomes a building, and so becomes part of history. I think the juxtaposition of the light frame and the solid, heavy stone building somehow points a way to an easily changed, elegant architecture, and I am interested in putting these things together.

TRACES OF HISTORY RETAINED +
ANNOTATED
R.H. DEC. 78'

THE NOTEBOOKS

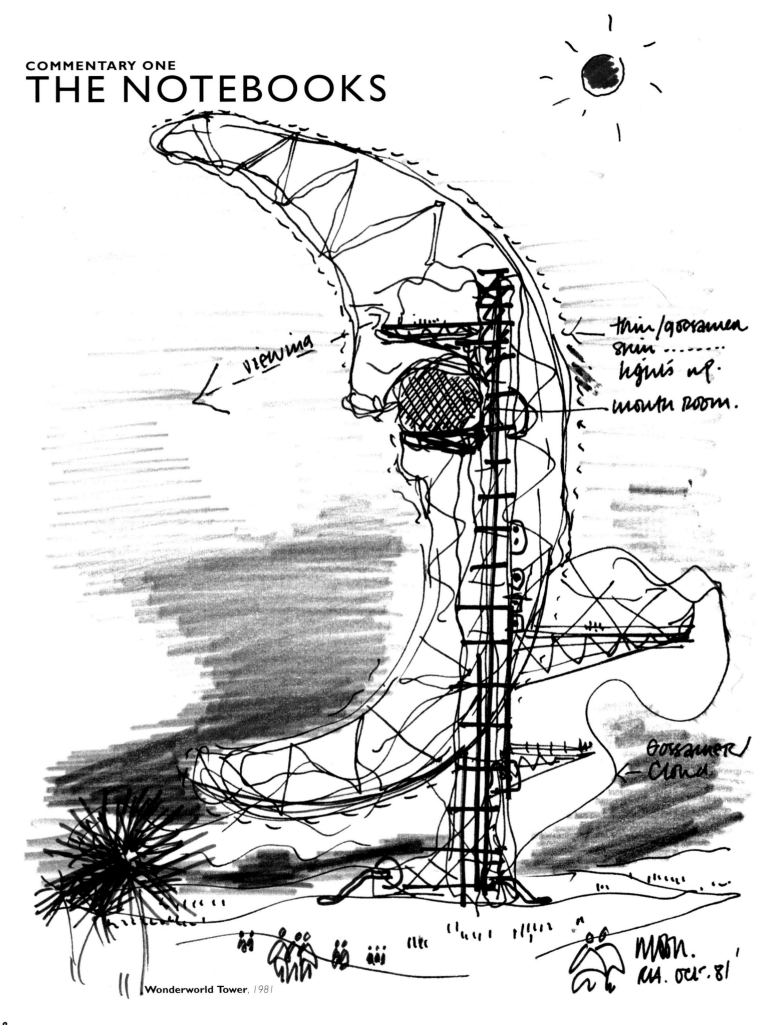

Wonderworld Tower, 1981

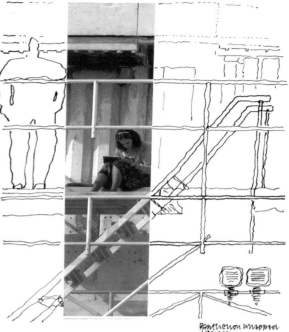

Panthenon wrapped + accessed.
July 87.

The PANTHENON accessed.

virtual olympics
7.9.92

RON HERRON DOES NOT 'DRAW LIKE AN ANGEL' (presumably with a quill plucked from its own wings?), but like a human being, which is a lot more interesting; and like an architect, which is what interests us here. Superficially, architects draw in any number of styles, and more profoundly every architect has his own signature style, so that one can tell a Peruzzi from a Palladio, or a Graves from a Hejduk, and can usually tell the members of Archigram from one another. But architects' drawings as a class or sub-culture are unlike even other classes of drawing made in the same orthogonal, axonometric or perspective conventions by, for instance, mechanical engineers.

Although the drawings of some engineers are very beautiful, they remain in intention purely instrumental, simply procedures for getting things done (or so most engineers would have us believe). The drawings of architects, on the other hand, are much less purely instrumental, and quite often have nothing to do with getting anything done at all. Rather, they are imbued with meanings over and above what they appear to show, and express a value system that is peculiar to architects. But different architects attribute the most important meanings and values to different classes of drawings – for some it will be rendered perspectives, for others it will be the first scratchings of the basic *parti*. For the Stirling office for many years it was the isometrics made to monitor the design while it was in process; for Corbu it was probably the drawings made while on his feet to illustrate lectures.

VIRTUAL OLYMPICS
Television is taking over sport so why not move the Olympics into the world of virtual reality – completely.
In the virtual world, the Olympics could always take place in Olympia and the marathon at Marathon, but in effect be organised anywhere and everywhere. No arguing about the venue… No need to travel, build stadia, accommodation, pools and velodromes. The virtual world – like the virtual world of television – takes over.

Arguably, Ron Herron's most revealing drawings are those in the black bound notebooks he has been keeping since around 1978. They are of large and small format, though none are larger than quarto/A4, and they cover overlapping periods of one or two years each. Their contents are extremely various. Some represent early sketches for real projects – allowing that the word 'real' has to have a very variable consistency here, ranging from exhibitions that happened to theme parks that didn't. Others are just thinking out loud or records of things seen. Many deal with obsessive inventions, usually robotic devices and mechanical arms and articulated equipments. And a late set points towards the Robohouse and Studio Strip House concepts that finally became the video that was shown in the *VISION DER MODERNE* exhibition in Frankfurt in 1986.

But in spite of the diversity of aims and topics, there is a great consistency about the contents of almost a decade of these notebooks. The obvious source of that consistency is in the drawing, in the evenness of the line and the regularity of its shaping. The R50 Pentel ballpen moves over the surface of the paper without hesitation or directional emphasis, as precise or imprecise as it needs to be – a page where all straight lines are wiggly will also contain a couple of (move over, Giotto!) almost perfect circles drawn

THE HUMAN STORY

This was a travelling exhibition on the story of mankind, as told by the paleoanthropologist Richard Leakey, which went around Europe – Amsterdam, Stockholm, Paris, London. From our point of view the interesting thing was making sure that the exhibition got across this extraordinary story, which began with the formation of the earth and moved through the various known phases of development to the present day. Many of the exhibits were constructed as computer models. One looked, for example, at hip joints, comparing the different movements of early man and ape. (The great thing about these exhibitions is that you become an instant authority on the subject. Of course, all that knowledge goes away again very quickly.) A lot of the story was told by video images transferred through the computer: there were some hands-on tools and interactive touch screens where you could ask questions and get answers. To represent the huge leaps through millions of years, we used little time boxes as a sort of time warp element between different parts of the exhibition. There were also a number of dioramas, a Victorian museum device, but we dealt with them rather like movie-sets. One rather amusing exhibit was a life-size model of Lucy, the famous upright link in the evolutionary chain. Lucy was very important, but she was rather small and we felt she looked rather boring, just standing there with a trail of footprints behind her. Leakey suggested that we made the eyes of the model move, and we did – but only once every fifteen minutes so that people were never quite sure if they were imagining things or not.

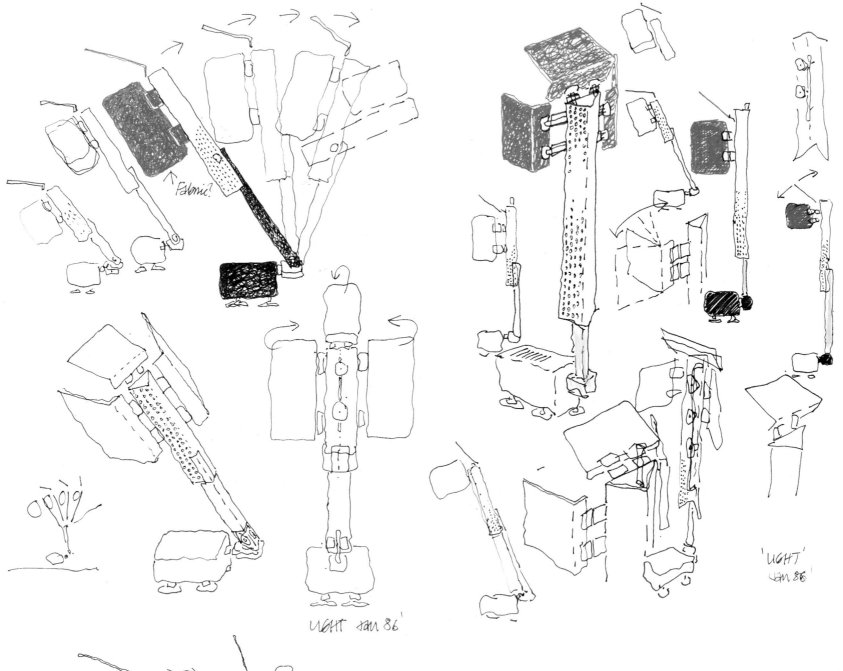

'LIGHT Jan 86'

'LIGHT Jan 86'

free-hand. The actual quality of the line and its shaping may resemble, if it resembles anything, that of Cedric Price or of Birkin Haward while in Norman Foster's office, but that may just be the temper of the times and the capacities of the drawing instruments – you can still be pretty sure which drawing is by Herron. The implicit signature is clear.

The other source of consistency is a matter of quite a different order; the drawings in the sketchbook seem to represent the same creative moment, the moment of the capture of the idea, perhaps even the *process* of its capture. Where two or three drawings on the same theme occur on successive pages – the 'Light' sequence in the 1986 quarto notebook, for instance – one can see refinement and revision, but one can also see the whole concept firmly nailed down for the first time. With most architects there is usually a sheaf of spoilers and abandoned versions before the sketch where it finally comes together. Not, it seems, with Ron Herron – there is hardly a crossed-out drawing or torn-out page in the whole sequence of notebooks. In these half-dozen black bound volumes you see, with extraordinary consistency, not the process of design, but the fixing of the concept designed. These are not drawings of searching or becoming; these are drawings of having got it right.

Millnenton – signs/video screens.

Hamburg.
28·8·87.

Plan – + Hotel/Kopfbern
+ Museum Tower.
expanded plan

HAMBURG LAND PIER

In 1987 Peter Cook, Christine Hawley and I were invited to take part in a competition for the rejuvenation of the decaying docks area half a mile or so from the centre of Hamburg. The competition organisers were really looking for a conference centre on a particular site, but we happened to misunderstand the briefing (because our German wasn't up to it) and became fascinated instead with the idea of tying the waterfront back into the centre of the city with a thing we called the Land Pier. This was a sort of 1960s deck revisited, except this time we used the Pier as a linking armature to pick up a series of events designed to commemorate the 500th anniversary of the docks. We proposed a route stretching from the docks to the end of the Reeperbahn, with conference centres, a museum, small concert hall, amphitheatre, bars, temporary exhibition buildings, railway stations, restaurants, and so on. On its way to the centre, the Land Pier went through a valley and in to a park area, where it flew along at tree-top level – an extraordinary experience reminiscent of the Battersea tree walk of 1951. Escalators with retractable covers provided a link down to the ground. The Land Pier would have truly fingered into the mettle of Hamburg.

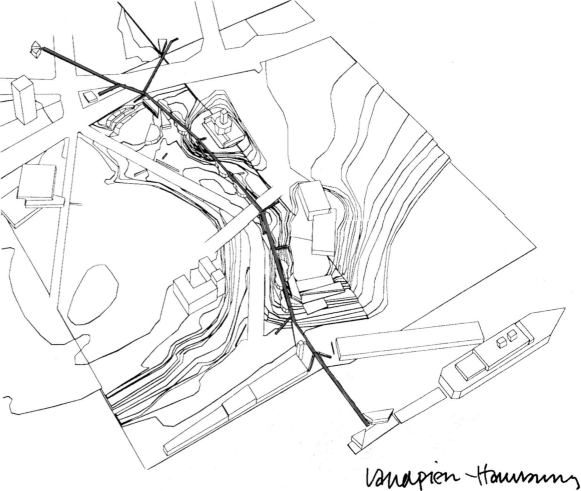

Landpier Hamburg

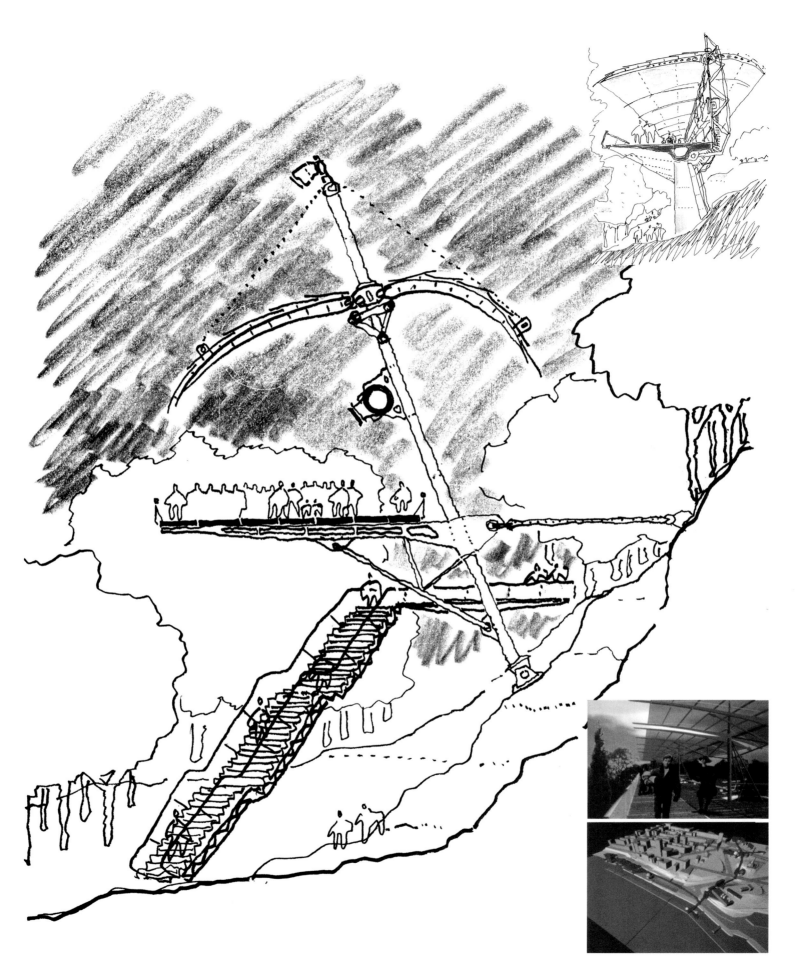

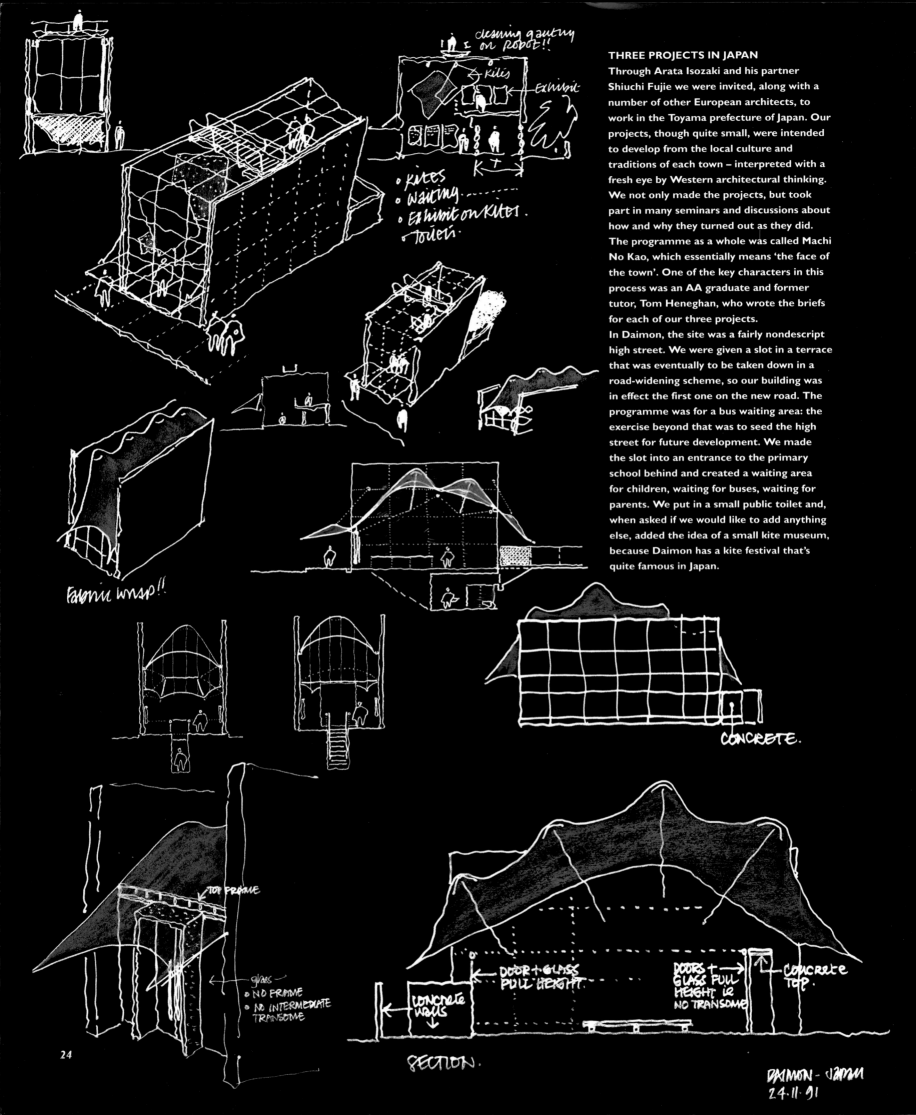

THREE PROJECTS IN JAPAN

Through Arata Isozaki and his partner Shiuchi Fujie we were invited, along with a number of other European architects, to work in the Toyama prefecture of Japan. Our projects, though quite small, were intended to develop from the local culture and traditions of each town – interpreted with a fresh eye by Western architectural thinking. We not only made the projects, but took part in many seminars and discussions about how and why they turned out as they did. The programme as a whole was called Machi No Kao, which essentially means 'the face of the town'. One of the key characters in this process was an AA graduate and former tutor, Tom Heneghan, who wrote the briefs for each of our three projects.

In Daimon, the site was a fairly nondescript high street. We were given a slot in a terrace that was eventually to be taken down in a road-widening scheme, so our building was in effect the first one on the new road. The programme was for a bus waiting area: the exercise beyond that was to seed the high street for future development. We made the slot into an entrance to the primary school behind and created a waiting area for children, waiting for buses, waiting for parents. We put in a small public toilet and, when asked if we would like to add anything else, added the idea of a small kite museum, because Daimon has a kite festival that's quite famous in Japan.

- kites
- waiting
- Exhibit on kites.
- toilets.

Fabric wrap!!

CONCRETE.

TOP FRAME

glass
- NO FRAME
- NO INTERMEDIATE TRANSOME

DOOR + GLASS FULL HEIGHT.

DOORS + GLASS FULL HEIGHT ie NO TRANSOME

CONCRETE TOP.

CONCRETE WALLS

SECTION.

DAIMON – JAPAN
24.11.91

24

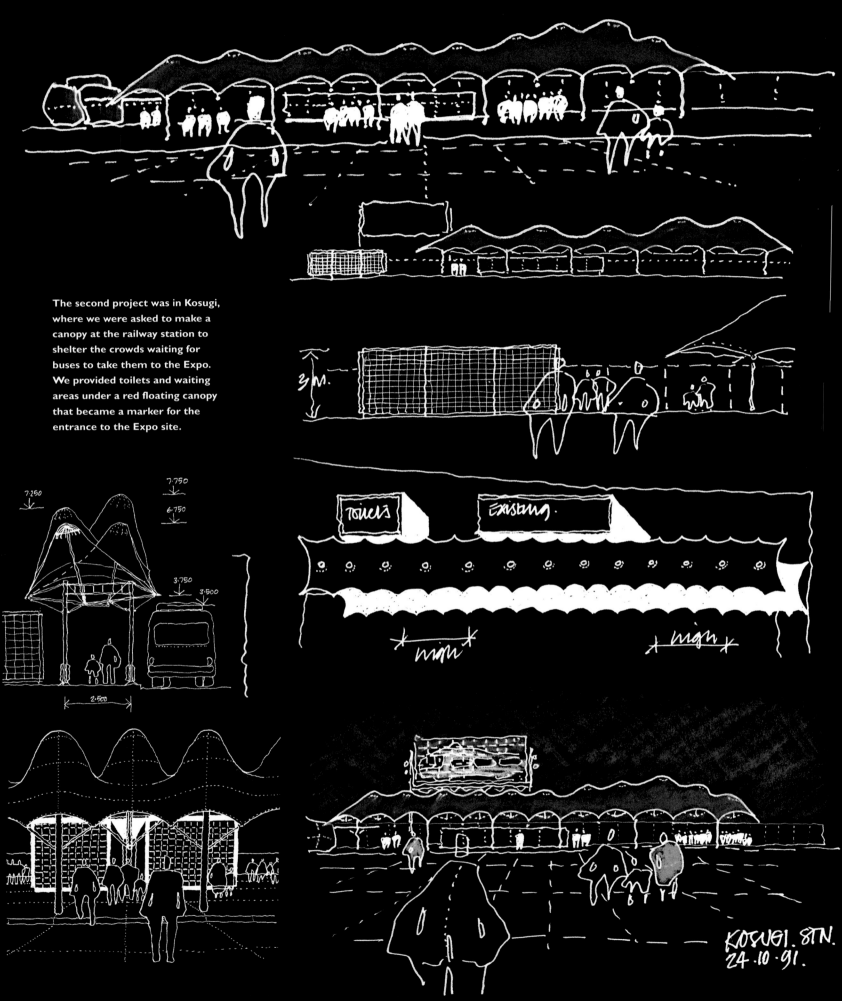

The second project was in Kosugi, where we were asked to make a canopy at the railway station to shelter the crowds waiting for buses to take them to the Expo. We provided toilets and waiting areas under a red floating canopy that became a marker for the entrance to the Expo site.

KOSUGI. STN.
24.10.91.

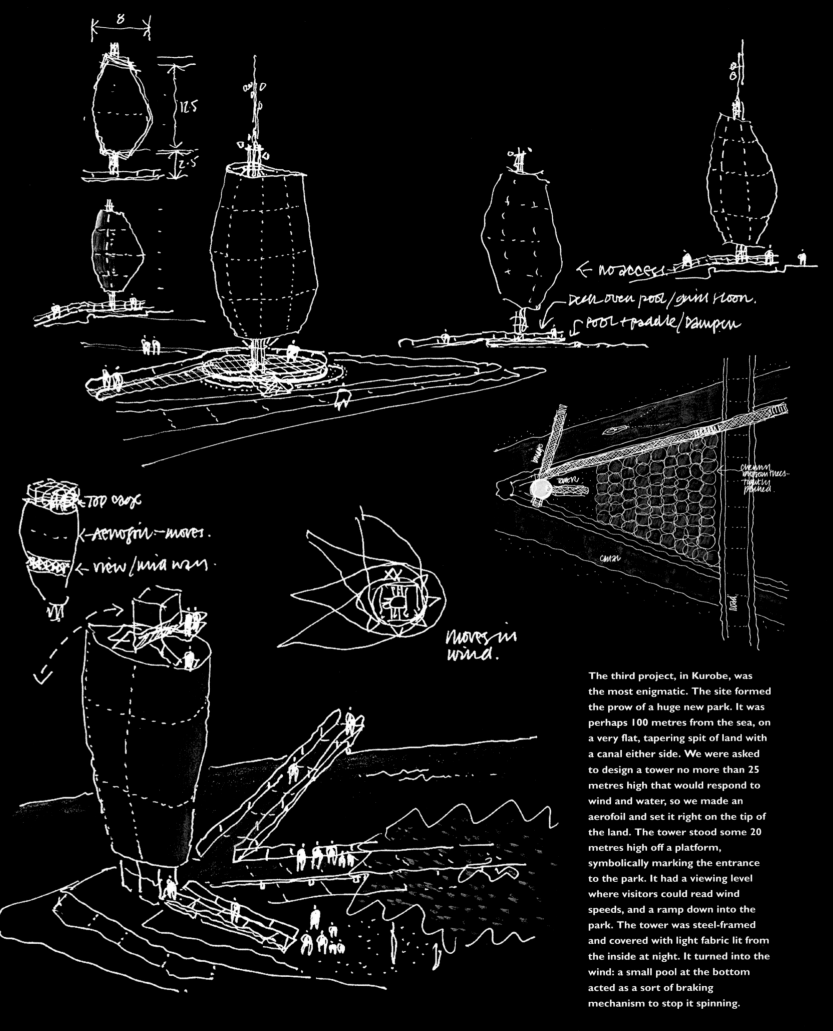

The third project, in Kurobe, was the most enigmatic. The site formed the prow of a huge new park. It was perhaps 100 metres from the sea, on a very flat, tapering spit of land with a canal either side. We were asked to design a tower no more than 25 metres high that would respond to wind and water, so we made an aerofoil and set it right on the tip of the land. The tower stood some 20 metres high off a platform, symbolically marking the entrance to the park. It had a viewing level where visitors could read wind speeds, and a ramp down into the park. The tower was steel-framed and covered with light fabric lit from the inside at night. It turned into the wind: a small pool at the bottom acted as a sort of braking mechanism to stop it spinning.

IMAGINATION

Over a three- to four-year period prior to moving to Store Street, the design company Imagination looked at a number of possibilities for larger premises. The first of these was on Canary Wharf around 1980, prior to the Reichmann development. We were going to build a steel frame structure off the basic foundations of an old banana warehouse to make an adaptable building that opened out at either end into external spaces for events and the making of films, videos and sets.

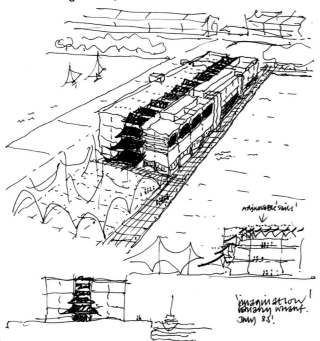

After this I looked at a project on a site behind the Round House in Camden Town, an area locked in by the canal and railway. The much more ambitious proposition there was to make an 'Imagination City', similar to 20th Century Fox, with film and video studios, sound recording places, set-making, fashion houses and design studios. The project included an area for the construction of sound stages and film-sets which was just a steel frame, a rolling roof and drivable walls, and so could be pulled back and adapted, expanded and contracted at will.

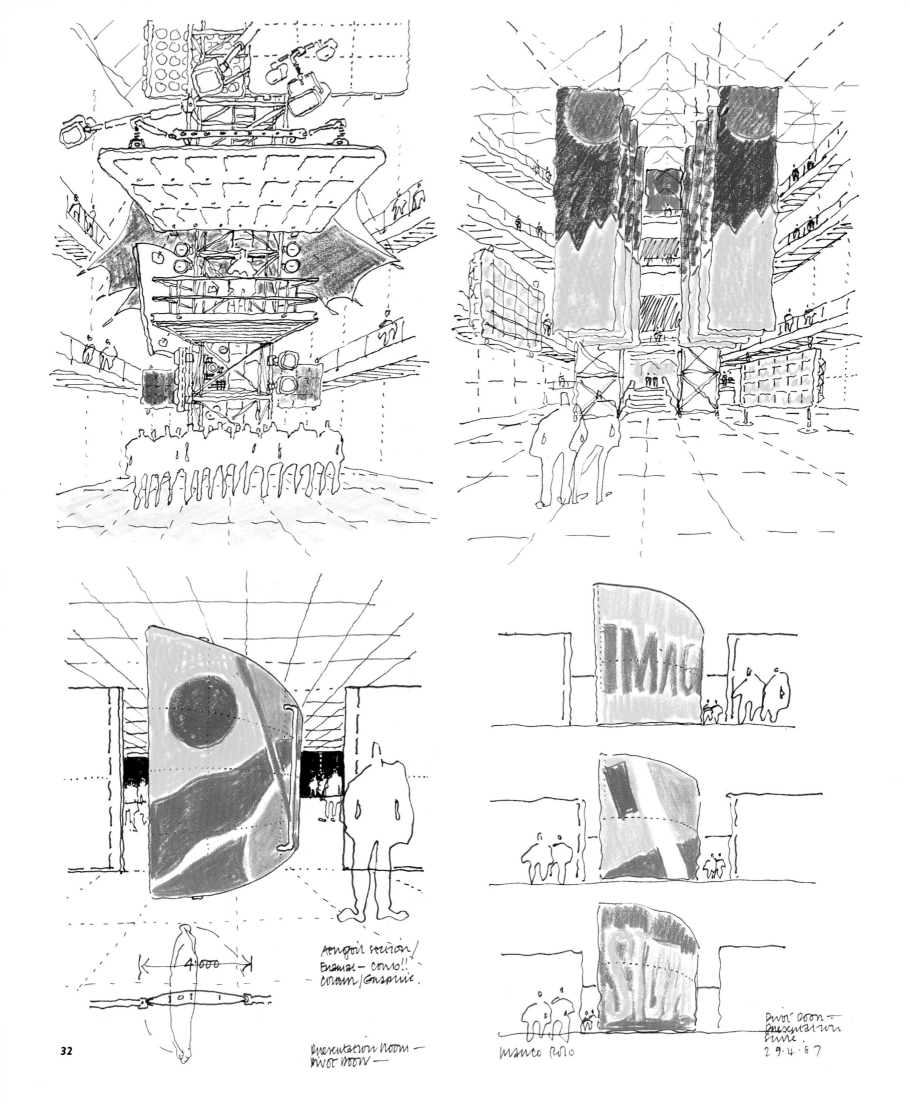

32

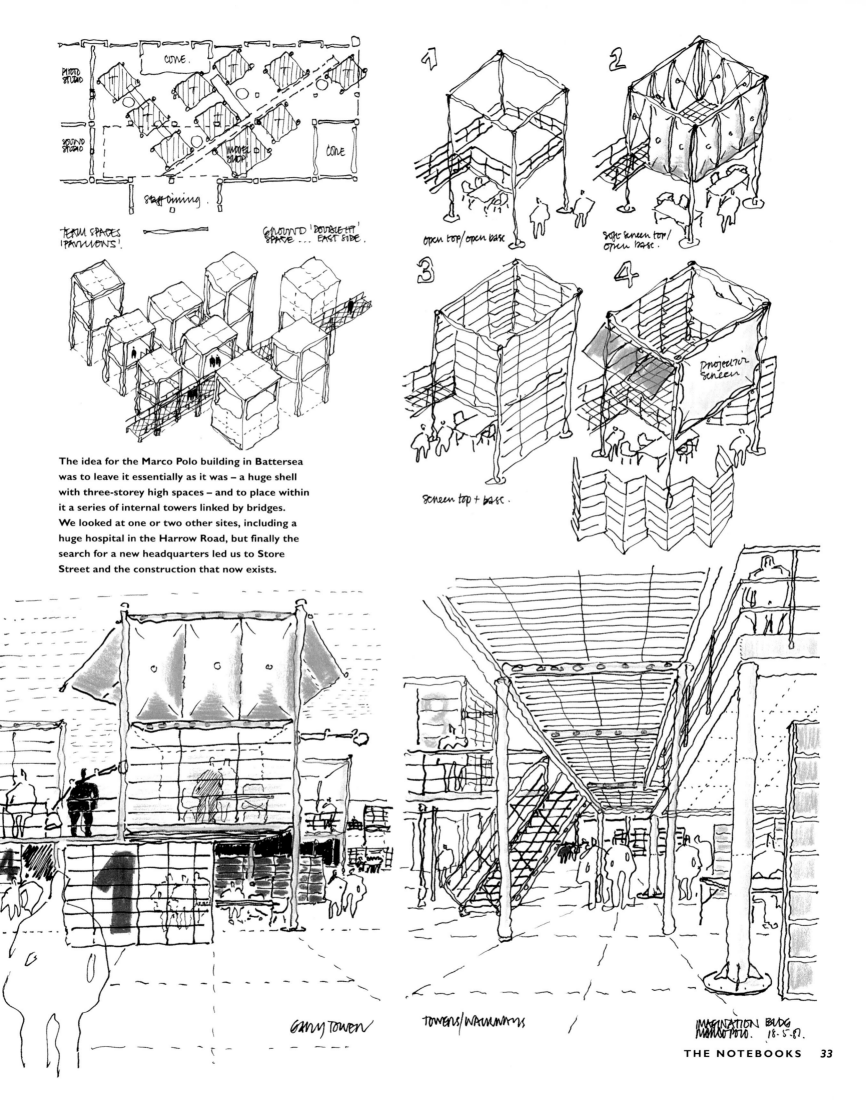

The idea for the Marco Polo building in Battersea was to leave it essentially as it was – a huge shell with three-storey high spaces – and to place within it a series of internal towers linked by bridges. We looked at one or two other sites, including a huge hospital in the Harrow Road, but finally the search for a new headquarters led us to Store Street and the construction that now exists.

1 STREET.

2 ENTRM.

3 THE PLACE

STORE STREET

As an architect working in London, I suppose it's inevitable that I am fascinated by the possibilities of adding to or altering the existing fabric, particularly in the areas between buildings. This was something I pursued in the 1970s, notably in the Tuning London project of 1972 and the Insertions projects of 1977.

An opportunity finally came to test these ideas when I was asked by Imagination to look at a possible new headquarters building in Store Street. When we visited the site we discovered that the building was an H-plan arrangement, consisting of two long blocks linked in the centre by a block with courtyard lightwells either side. It was obvious that there was great potential for using the area between the two blocks to make a new kind of events space – a space that could be changed, reconstructed, re-lit, re-presented over time.

We initially looked at putting a glass roof over the space. This didn't work: the two blocks were not exactly parallel, so we ended up with distorted roof shapes. Then I had the idea of wrapping the central area in a fabric structure – rather like Christo might. It seemed to be a slightly crazy idea, so I tried it out on my son, Andrew, who is my partner, thinking that if he thought it was all right, it probably was. I showed him a very rough sketch that I'd made and his immediate reaction was 'Let's go for it'. So we set about trying to make it work.

link + light

imagination bldg.
store st.
5.1.88.

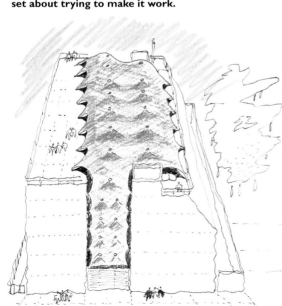

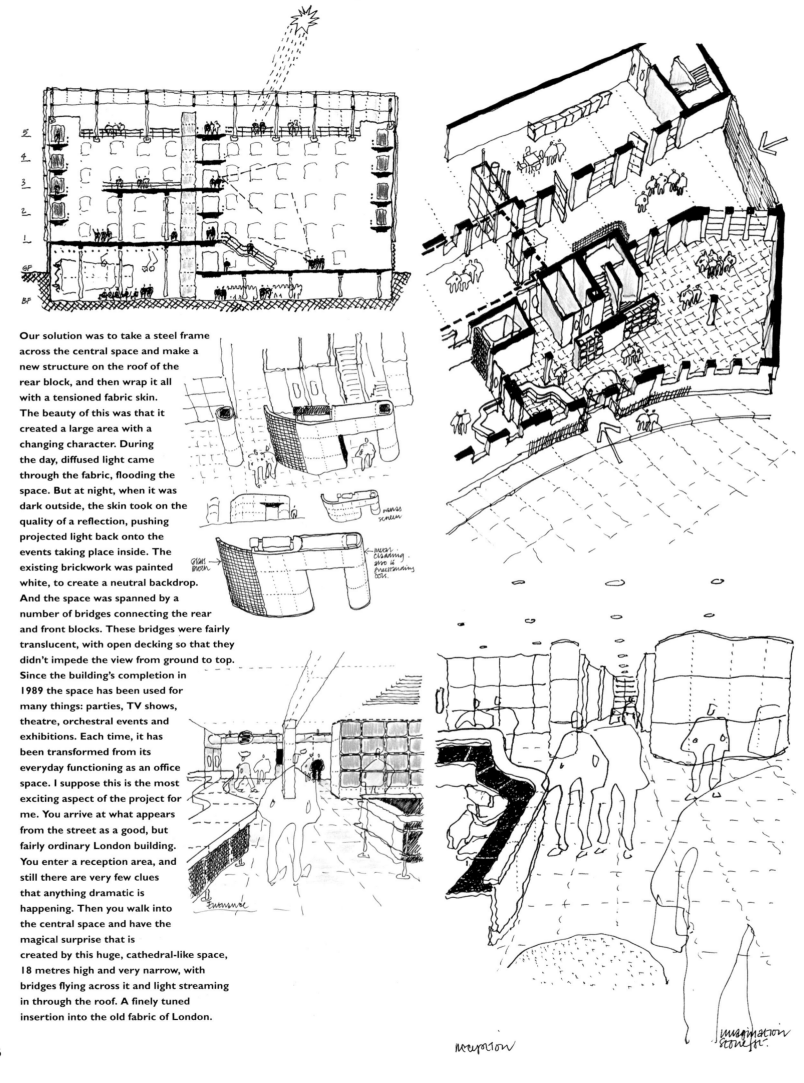

Our solution was to take a steel frame across the central space and make a new structure on the roof of the rear block, and then wrap it all with a tensioned fabric skin. The beauty of this was that it created a large area with a changing character. During the day, diffused light came through the fabric, flooding the space. But at night, when it was dark outside, the skin took on the quality of a reflection, pushing projected light back onto the events taking place inside. The existing brickwork was painted white, to create a neutral backdrop. And the space was spanned by a number of bridges connecting the rear and front blocks. These bridges were fairly translucent, with open decking so that they didn't impede the view from ground to top. Since the building's completion in 1989 the space has been used for many things: parties, TV shows, theatre, orchestral events and exhibitions. Each time, it has been transformed from its everyday functioning as an office space. I suppose this is the most exciting aspect of the project for me. You arrive at what appears from the street as a good, but fairly ordinary London building. You enter a reception area, and still there are very few clues that anything dramatic is happening. Then you walk into the central space and have the magical surprise that is created by this huge, cathedral-like space, 18 metres high and very narrow, with bridges flying across it and light streaming in through the roof. A finely tuned insertion into the old fabric of London.

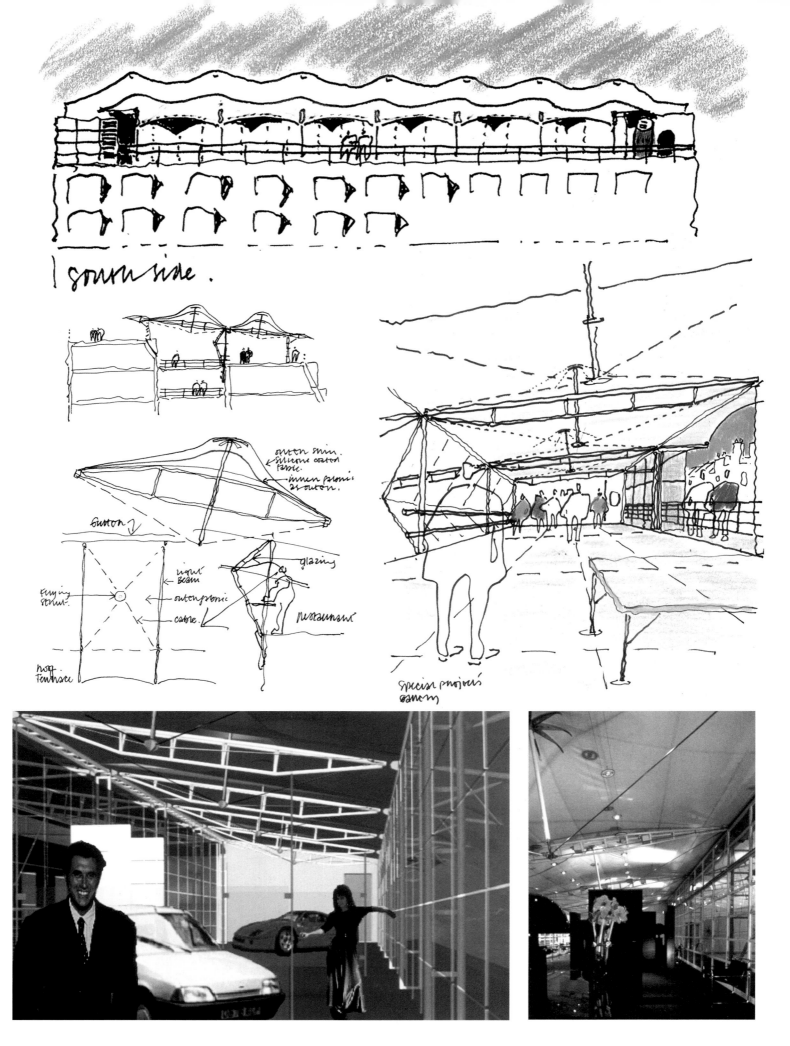

south side.

outer skin.
silicone coated fabric.
inner ptonic as outer.

button

flying strut.

light beam
outer ptonic
cable.

glazing

restaurant

roof
penthse.

special projects
gallery

COMMENTARY TWO
LOOSE PACKAGES

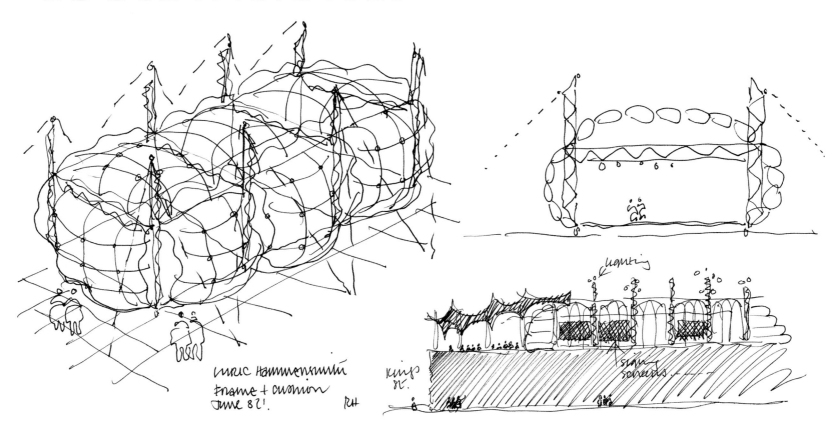

THROUGHOUT RON HERRON'S NOTEBOOKS, in particular, there runs a particular strain of imagery in which the actual envelope that encloses the usable space of the proposed building looks as if it has been crammed loosely and baggily into a regular, rigid, rectangular frame, between whose stiff members the enclosing envelope bulges like – dare one say it? – the overstuffed cushions of one of Le Corbusier's heroically uncomfortable *Fauteuils Grand Confort*. One may dare just say that, because on one of the relevant sketches, Herron actually uses the words 'cushion' and 'frame', only his come on more floppily, more sexily than Corb's.

But if the *Fauteuil Grand Confort* is indeed one of the buried sources that is tapped by, say, the Lyric Hammersmith sketches in the 1982 notebook, then it is only one among very many basic Modern Movement themes that is laid under tribute here, wittingly or otherwise. For this is the classic Modernist frame-and-fill concept of building, inherited from the theories of Viollet-le-Duc via the concrete-framed practices of Auguste Perret, proudly realised in the glass and steel facades of Miesian towers as well as in the cruddy old hollow tiles that filled between the frames of Corbusian buildings where frame and fill alike were concealed by an eye-soothing poultice of plasterwork. The concept was rediscovered by the Japanese Metabolists and megastructuralists everywhere, in the concept of a giant urban frame (Habraken's Dragers, or supports) infilled with whole dwellings or Archigram-style capsules. Within the Herron circle and generation, its revival is probably due to Mike Webb's famous thesis project, with its bulging Bowellist accommodations carried in a structural grid of the most prissily rectilinear aspect, and thoroughly enjoying the almost surrealist implications of this confrontation of the bulgy and the stiff.

If the Herron version is more of the same out of that tradition, with the fill reduced to

INFLATABLES
The Cardiff Airhouse project of 1965 (below) was a proposal for a small exhibition at Cardiff Castle. It was my first foray into pneumatics, a soft, friendly space that oozed out of the ramparts of the heavy, solid castle. This interest in inflatables – the idea of a skin into which you just put air to make a space – has

mere plastic membranes, it has an observational source as well: the notebooks frequently record the aspect of building sites when they are well up, and the risen grids of the scaffolding have been loosely hung about with fabric weather-protection for the workforce. The back influence on modes of architectural vision of building sites while the structure is 'in the process of becoming' is a topic that works like the Pompidou Centre and Lloyd's of London make ripe for study – and sketches like these suggest some good places for that study to begin.

But these sketches of Ron Herron's are also somewhat Modern Movement classics in themselves, flash-gun marriages of theory and observation rendered memorable by draftsmanship so improvisatory that it could only have been produced by a lifetime of practised skill. And behind that lies the echo of yet another Modern Movement classic; Walter Gropius' Zen-style maxim: 'Master an infallible technique – and then forget about it!' – and how different the Modern Movement might have looked if only W.G. himself had ever managed to live up to that ideal! But in this seemingly casual, perfectly controlled, economical and punishingly precise style of drawing one can see epitomised a large part of the Herron approach – that part which depends upon long-accumulated experience and the trained habits of converting it into graphic form, of making architecture of it on the page under the fast-moving point of the practised pen that never needs to go back and correct or erase. The loose packages in the notebooks prove to contain more than meets the eye; behind their floppy forms lies a whole history, full of Modernist allusion, and eloquent proof that the architecture of 'that Old Modern Movement' lives because, far from being reductionist or merely instrumental, it comes loaded with the experience and the aspirations of the weird civilisation we have come to inhabit.

led me into a number of projects since: the **Seaside Bubbles, Airhab, the Slug, the Bubble Theatre, and the Lyric Theatre in Hammersmith. At the Lyric, I was asked to make a rehearsal room on the flat roof outside the foyer of the existing theatre. It was a temporary space, as planning laws practically ruled out a permanent building on the roof. To make the structure as light as possible, we chose to use an aluminium frame with inflatable bags as cladding within the frame. The frames were wedged down on to the roof structure, up against the existing building. The bulbous, slug-like temporary structure then just sat on the roof and almost oozed over the edge.**

BERLIN SETS

The Aedus Gallery in Berlin set a competition which asked people to react to the fact that Hugh Stubbins Congress Building of 1958 had collapsed. I made a new Congress Building that was inflatable, and called it Soft Collapse. Within the 'soft' structure, 'Sets Fit for Berlin' responds to events, whether congress, concert, exhibition, movie, banquet, or summer restaurant under the spare-ribs – A Public 'Set'.

'Soft' venue
'Berlin Sets'

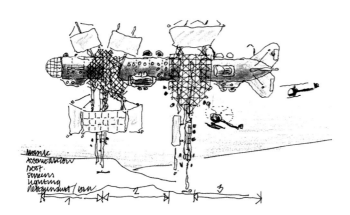

INSTANT CITY AIRSHIPS

In the early 1970s, as part of the Instant City project, both Peter Cook and I designed airships. We were inspired, I think, by all the discussion in the press at the time about the possibility of using airships as cargo-carrying devices. My version was a really huge airship that quietly floated in to create a place for events like Woodstock. The airship deployed a platform which hovered over the ground. It dropped screens and lifts and a video wall and a cover to make a huge floating auditorium. And, like the Instant City, when it had completed the event, it would lift up its skirts and move on to the next venue.

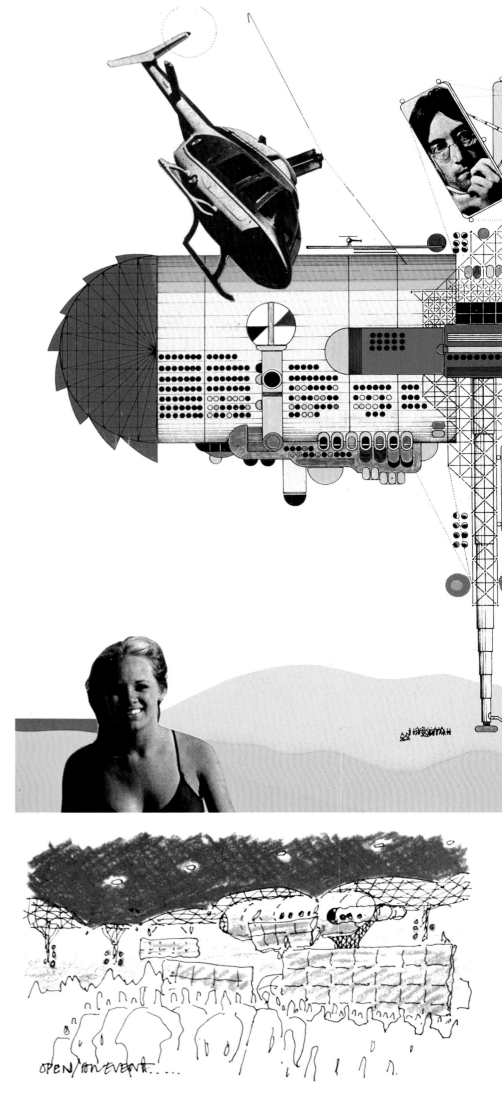

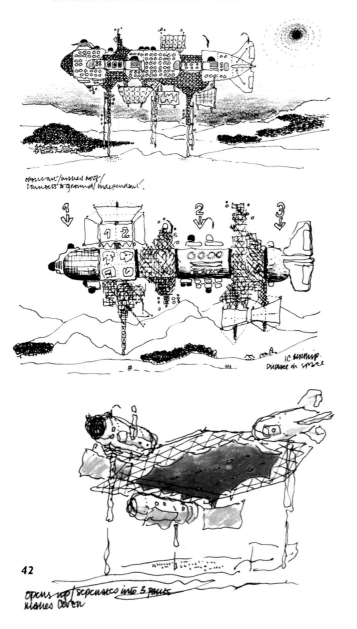

42

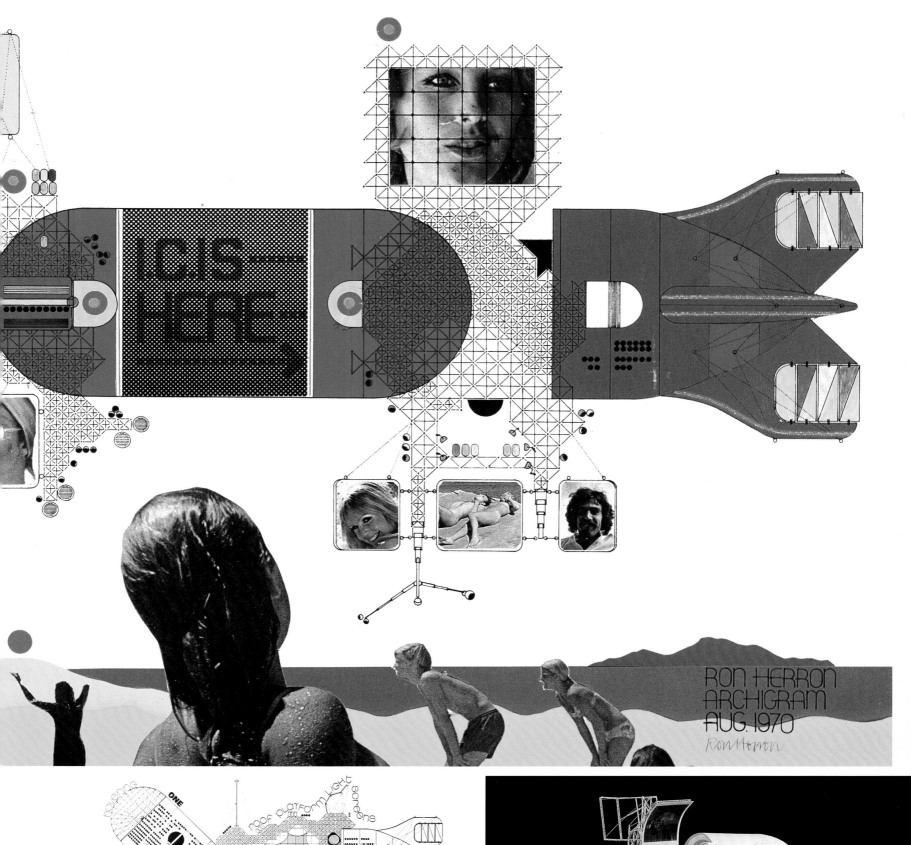

IT IS ... HERE

RON HERRON
ARCHIGRAM
AUG. 1970

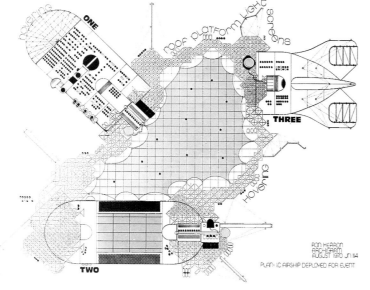

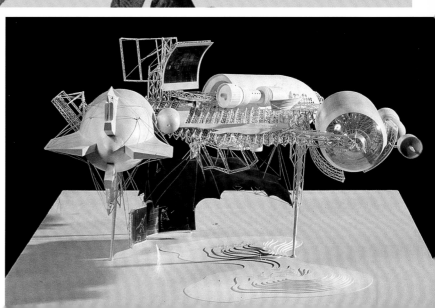

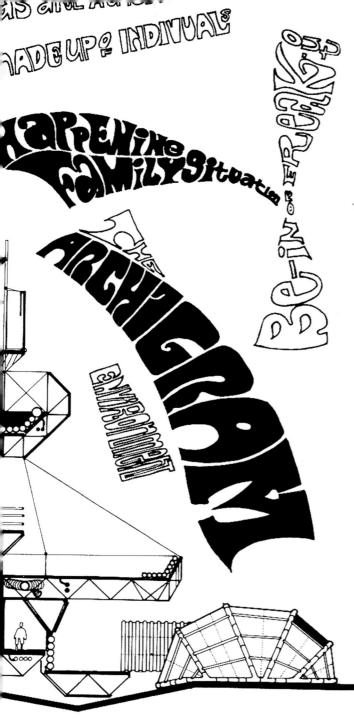

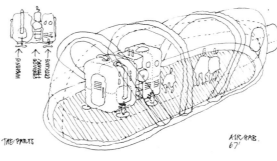

THE PARTS   AIRHAB. 67'

Free-time - 68' RW.

CONTROL AND CHOICE

The Control and Choice project of 1966 was a combined effort by the Archigram group. It took the idea of a frame that stood in a normal city situation and looked at how it might be adapted to reflect the personalities of the users, the people living within the frame. There were many variations and parts that could be added or subtracted to make a personal environment. Control and Choice was about trying to invent a system that would allow freedom of choice but at the same time avoid the conflicts that cause a lot of open-ended projects to collapse.

One of the elements that I pursued as part of the Control and Choice project, but also separately, was a thing called Airhab. This was a kind of service trailer that you could pull behind a car; it was part bathroom, part kitchen or cooking area, part air supply transformer, and so on. You could also attach to it an inflatable, extendable space for camping or travelling. In the Control and Choice dwelling, the Airhab was a bedroom or study and a weekend space that could be trailed off into the countryside ... to gatherings of other Airhab users. The idea of the nomad was a predominant interest amongst everyone in the group at the time. A lot of these ideas about travelling grew into the project called Instant City, which we developed with a grant from the Graham Foundation. Instant City temporarily grafted the dynamic of the metropolitan scene on to a small local centre. It was sparked off largely by the big open-air rock concerts, like The Stones in Hyde Park, or Woodstock. But it also came out of our own travelling: we were lecturing and the Archigram Opera was touring the country like a circus. The design for Instant City brought together trailer units, inflatables, lightweight structures, gantries, towers, support systems, scaffolding, audio-visual displays, projection equipment and electronic display systems. The metropolis would arrive like the circus, set up shop, operate for a period of time, and then move on.

POPULAR PAK/TUNED SUBURBS

In 1968 Archigram was invited to make an installation at the Milan Triennale. The theme that year was the 'greater number problem', which Archigram, being much more optimistic than most, took as an advantage. We invented 'Popular Paks', packages of architecture which you could buy off the shelf and add to the existing environment to fine-tune it. A collage that I made for a project called Tuned Suburbs shows a fork-lift truck loaded with a Popular Pak driving into an invented suburb that is part Georgian, part Edwardian, part modern developer housing. The Popular Pak brought in elements to improve the environment – accretions of modern technology that showed how existing places could be tuned up, lifted to another dimension.

SIMULATION/TUNING LONDON

One of the long-standing interests that I share with Dennis Crompton is the idea of simulation, i.e. the simulation of reality. I suppose this fascination stemmed from looking at flight simulators which allowed you to fly an aeroplane and land at a particular airport without actually flying. The idea of going somewhere, but not going, inspired us to make simple simulations in a number of projects. We made a simulator for the Malaysian exhibition at the Commonwealth Institute in the early 1970s. And I made another in the late 1970s, in the Tuning London project, after seeing the movie *It's Tuesday, It Must Be Brussels*. The idea was for a place where visitors could see England through the centuries by means of simulation – where they could experience the Blitz, or the War of Roses, or travel around all the beauty spots without ever leaving the city.

I imagined the package tourists flying in and spending a day at the simulator and then flying off to Brussels… or perhaps not. Perhaps they could have done Brussels from the same location.

IT'S TUESDAY—IT MUST BE THAILAND!!

STIMULATION CENTRE

THEME PARKS

Over the past fifteen years or so I've
worked on a number of theme park
propositions. I suppose this is
something that developed out of living
in Los Angeles in the late 1960s,
because whenever friends from
Europe came to visit we'd go off to
Disneyland. Over a two-year period
I must have gone there, or to
20th Century Fox, some twenty
times. I became fascinated with
the idea of this sort of perfect
world; clean (particularly in the
Disney case), safe, with a fun
fair approach.

The first large theme park
that I was involved in was
Wonderworld in the north of
England, designed by Derek Walker
in the early 1980s. The landscape was
potentially beautiful, so my interest
was in using camouflage and movie-
set techniques to place the large
elements of the landscape discreetly
into the surroundings. I tried to get
away from the kind of roller coaster
or big wheel rides which most theme
parks still have as a legacy of the fun
fair by introducing the idea of
simulation. We simulated rock
climbing and beaches and space rides,
where the only movement was the
movement on the screen.

Wonderworld was based on a series of
fairy-tale, dream-like figures, so it lent
itself very well to simulation.

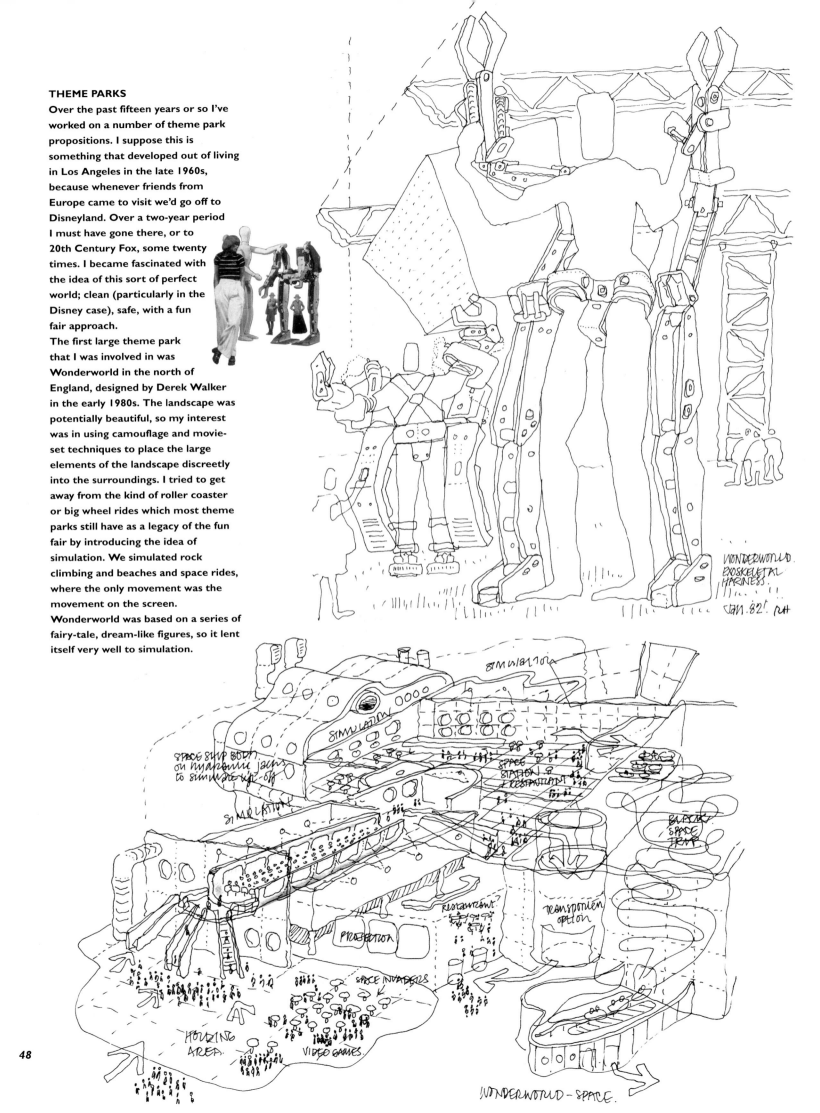

WONDERWORLD.
EXOSKELETAL
HARNESS.
Jan. 82. rH

WONDERWORLD - SPACE.

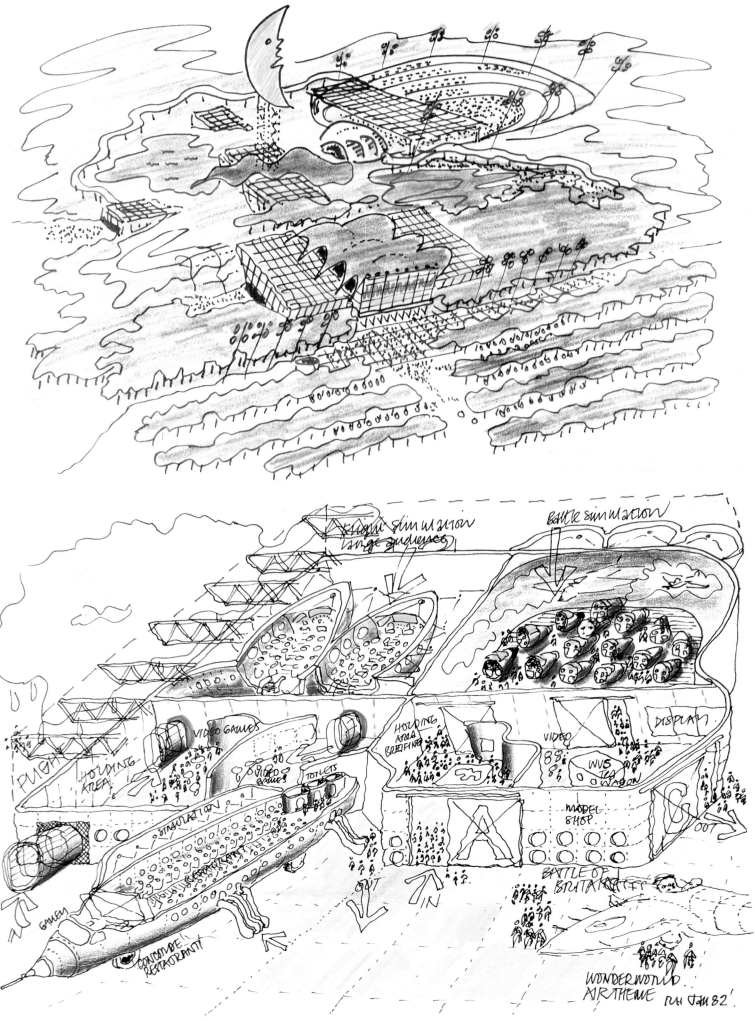

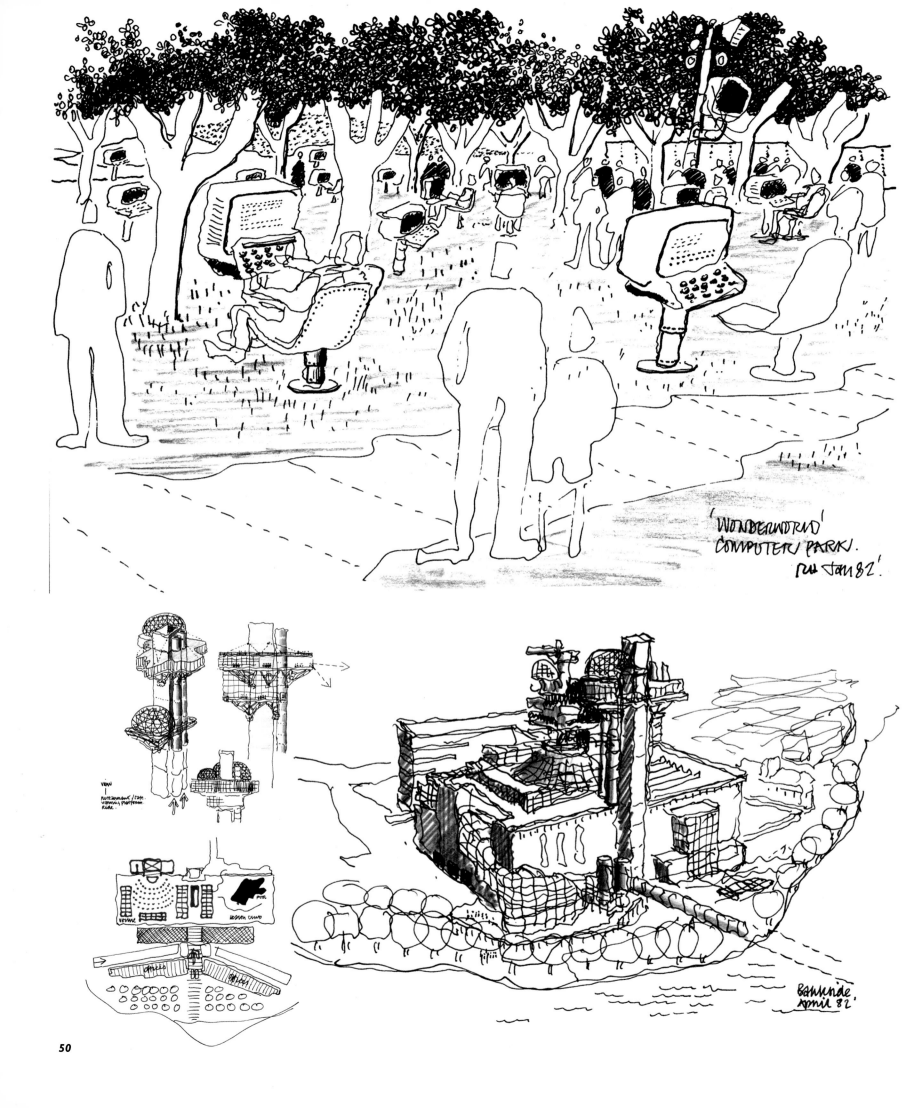

'WONDERWORLD'
COMPUTER PARK.
RW Jan 82'

Bankside
April 82'

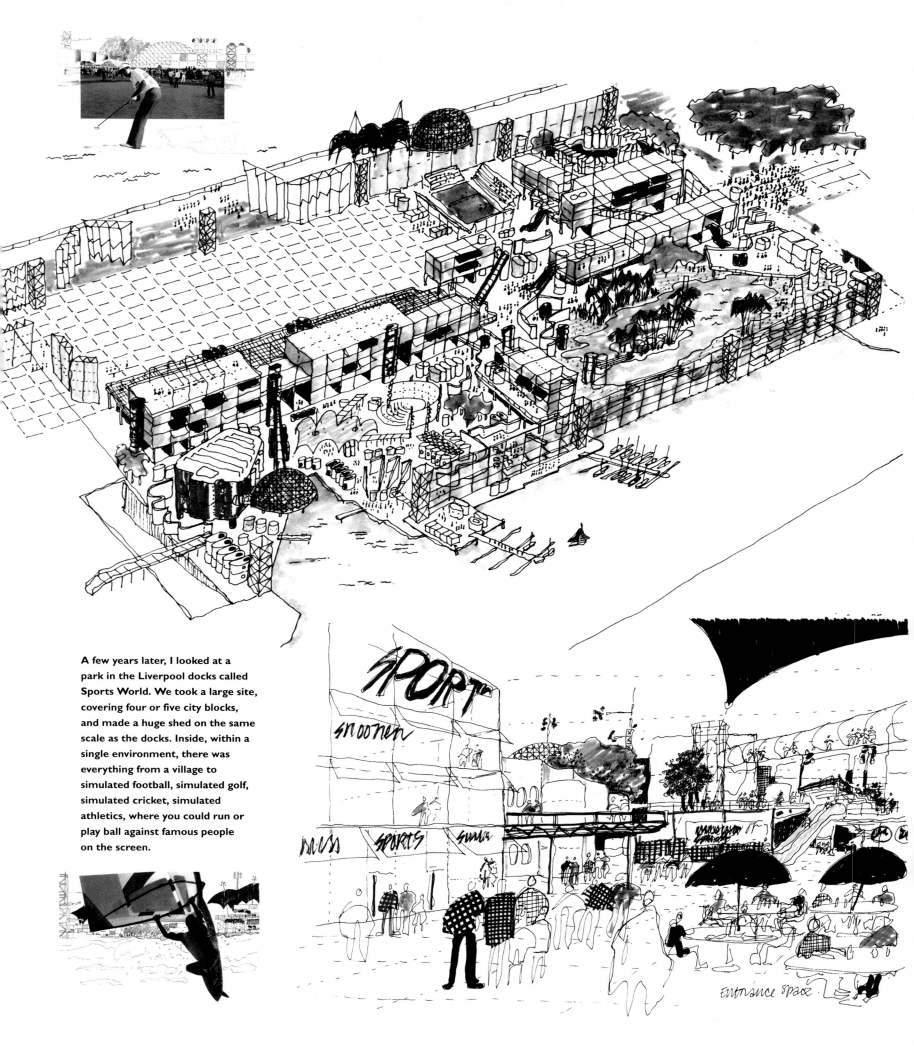

A few years later, I looked at a park in the Liverpool docks called Sports World. We took a large site, covering four or five city blocks, and made a huge shed on the same scale as the docks. Inside, within a single environment, there was everything from a village to simulated football, simulated golf, simulated cricket, simulated athletics, where you could run or play ball against famous people on the screen.

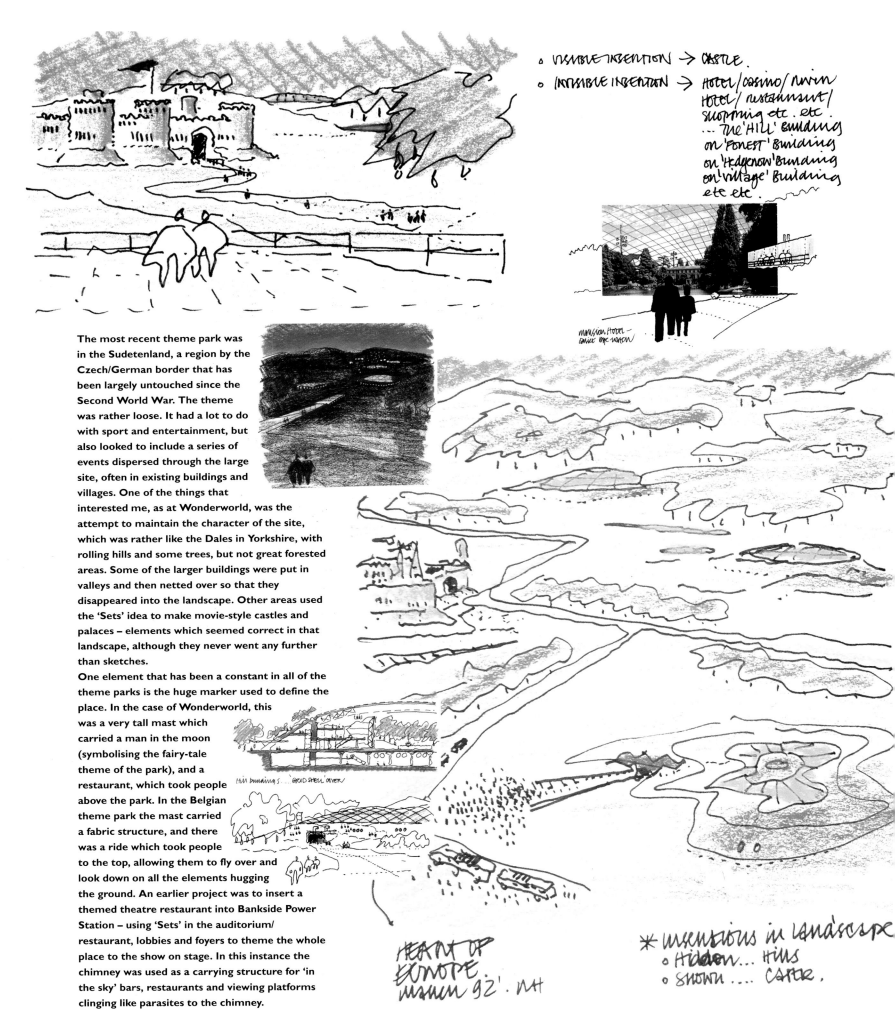

The most recent theme park was in the Sudetenland, a region by the Czech/German border that has been largely untouched since the Second World War. The theme was rather loose. It had a lot to do with sport and entertainment, but also looked to include a series of events dispersed through the large site, often in existing buildings and villages. One of the things that interested me, as at Wonderworld, was the attempt to maintain the character of the site, which was rather like the Dales in Yorkshire, with rolling hills and some trees, but not great forested areas. Some of the larger buildings were put in valleys and then netted over so that they disappeared into the landscape. Other areas used the 'Sets' idea to make movie-style castles and palaces – elements which seemed correct in that landscape, although they never went any further than sketches.

One element that has been a constant in all of the theme parks is the huge marker used to define the place. In the case of Wonderworld, this was a very tall mast which carried a man in the moon (symbolising the fairy-tale theme of the park), and a restaurant, which took people above the park. In the Belgian theme park the mast carried a fabric structure, and there was a ride which took people to the top, allowing them to fly over and look down on all the elements hugging the ground. An earlier project was to insert a themed theatre restaurant into Bankside Power Station – using 'Sets' in the auditorium/ restaurant, lobbies and foyers to theme the whole place to the show on stage. In this instance the chimney was used as a carrying structure for 'in the sky' bars, restaurants and viewing platforms clinging like parasites to the chimney.

'castle' - entry
insertions

'hotels in landscape'

'dancin' sec' - piazza

'station hotel - loading sec'

EXPAND/
CONTRACT   INFLATE
OPEN/CLOSED.

VIEW SET (Manhattan at night)

NIGHT
NIGHT   NIGHT   GUEST

CLOAK
POD

DAY   POOL   ST   DAY

VIEW SET (palms etc)

PAK-A-HOME
JULY 81.

CLOSE UP/COM
occupied/empty conditions

hinged
wall motorised

fold
hinge   open/
closed   open/
closed   variable

|←1→|←2|3→|←4→|←   8m   →|

DET: HOME: PAK—
VIEW SET!... DAY.

AUG. 81.

I wrote the following piece to go with my entry for the 1985 Shinkenchiku ideas competition for 'A House for the Year 2001', which I called 'Robohouse'.

A STYLE FOR THE YEAR 2001 – OR AN OPTIMIST'S VIEW OF THE FUTURE

It was 9pm on a cold winter's evening. The sky was dark and stormy, full of snow. I approached the house with great excitement. It appeared to dematerialise, it in indescribable colours, the light spread out and mixed with the night.

As I walked along the path, it glowed one metre ahead and one metre behind, following me as I walked. The front door slid open, emitting a warm, friendly, welcoming light. My host appeared at the opening and invited me in.

The lobby was like nothing I had ever seen. The walls were on the move, slowly taking up position, moving at the voice command of my host. A slow waltz of walls, screens, rooms and robotics. Silently and smoothly they moved into the positions they had learnt.

A small, friendly robot took my coat and hat, and moved quietly off to deposit them in a nearby container to be dried out and automatically pressed. The movement of elements finished, and the light programme began, the various surfaces taking up colours and textures – luminous effects from an interior source.

We stepped from the lobby into the living area. Another robot approached with a tray of drinks. My hostess rose to greet me from the soft area of the floor where she had been sitting. The floor subsided as she came towards me. We shook hands and she asked me to sit. As I sat back, an area of floor lifted to meet me and I sank into its soft, comfortable embrace.

I looked around me. The ceiling did not appear to exist. The stars shone in the dark sky; apparently there was no membrane between me and the heavens. My host asked if I would like to change the colours and positions of the various screens. I took up his offer. At my voice command the screens moved to the locations I requested. Almost imperceptibly, the colours changed from pink to blue, from white to orange. The video wall was playing out a recent concert, gently surrounding us with music.

We stepped out of the pool of sound and moved into the dining room. We sat, and were served by robots who had prepared the meal. The screens and lighting towers moved into positions they had learnt on a previous evening, to make a cosy, quiet enclosure. The effect of the whole was of a surface having within its molecular structure a source of light and colour.

After dinner we wandered around the house, moving rooms, screens and other elements at will, making enclosures and layering space, changing colour, surface and texture on command. The house was warm and friendy and totally responsive.

As I left, I reflected on the Robohouse. 'A style for the year 2001' is irrelevant. Style has always been irrelevant. The Robohouse is of its time. The past is only the starting point for the future.

As Albert Camus said, 'Style, like sheer silk, too

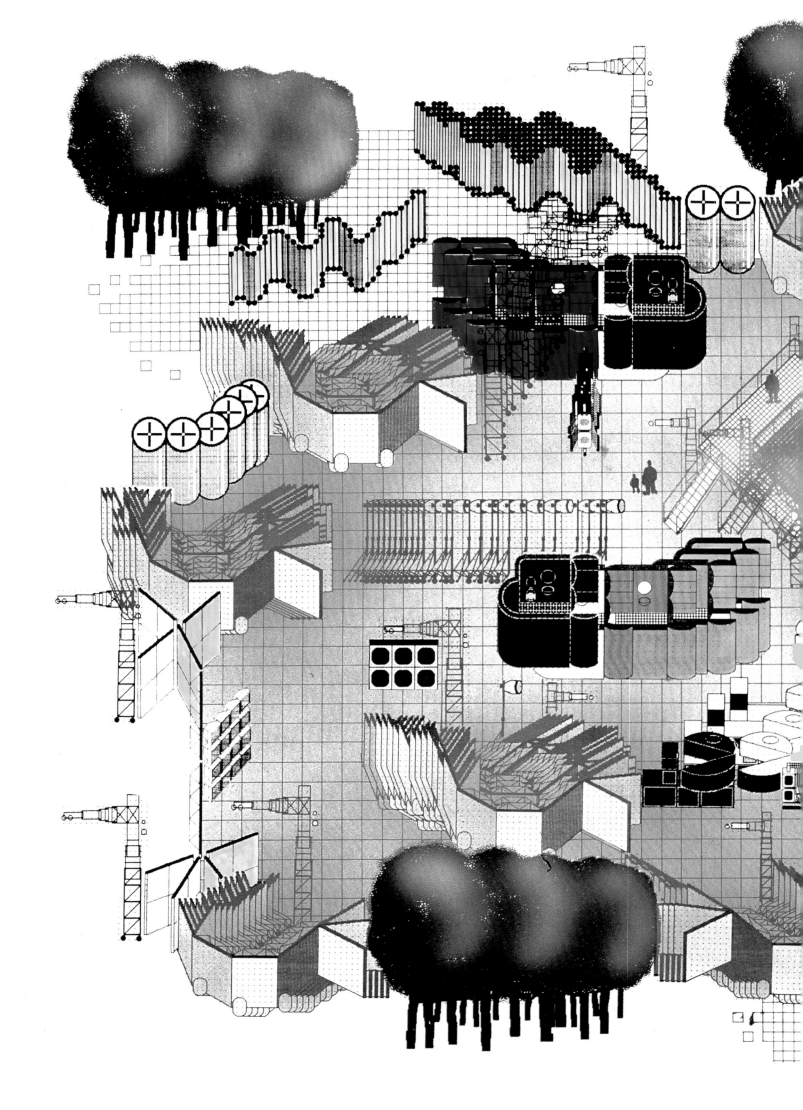

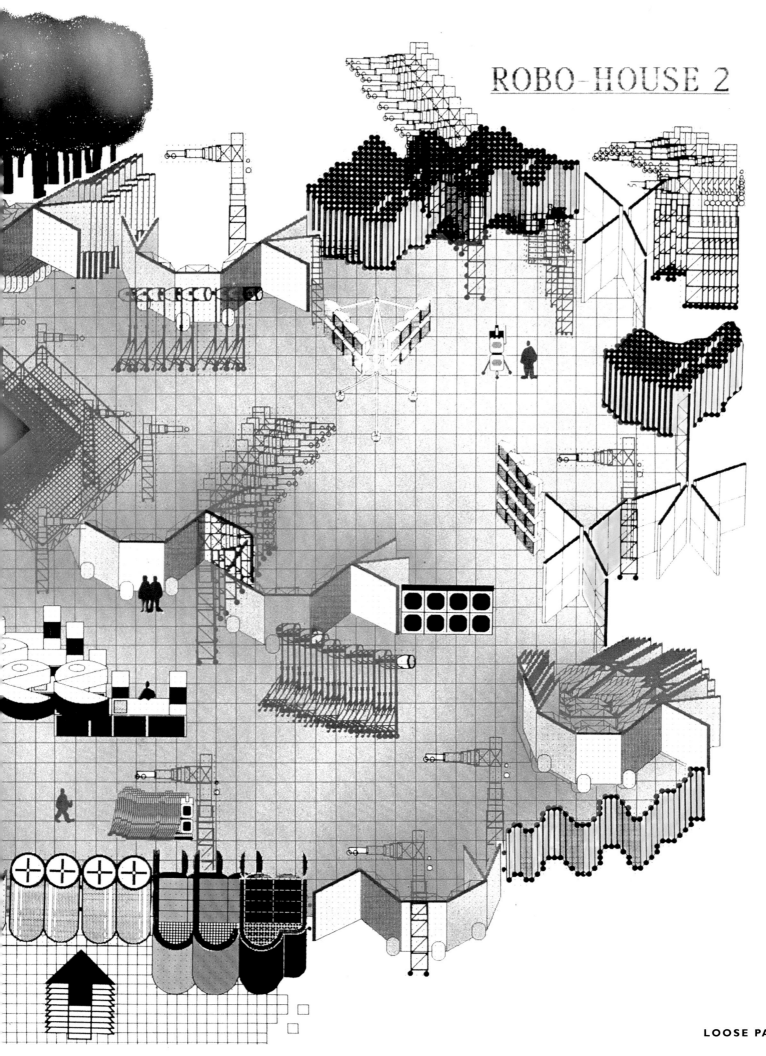

IT'S A.......? ......UNIVERSITY? AN ENTERTAINMENT FACILITY HOSING?

IT'S A.......

IT'S A........
RON HERRON
ARCHI

'IT'S A...'

In the early 1970s I read an article a British magazine deploring the fact that no style for a truly public architecture had evolved in modern times. I thought it rather amusing that someone could call for a style that represented 'public', or 'commercial', or whatever, and I made a project out of this, which really questioned labels. 'It's a...' said that if you put a sign saying 'hotel' or 'wax museum' on Buckingham Palace, it could very well be either. The only clue to its role as a palace were the soldiers marching up and down outside. There were other versions, like Westminster Abbey with an Odeon sign hung between the twin towers so that it became a cinema. The idea of labelling as an element of architecture took hold and I made a whole series of these joke demonstrations:

Is it a school?

Is it a public house?

Is it an office building?

What is it?

It's a...

ADD A LABEL—CHANGE THE SERVICING AND 'ITS A'.....?   RON HERRON 1974

PARK MOTEL

MOVIELAND WAX MUSEUM

Palace of Living Art

58

IT'S A?

IT'S A: NEW UNIVERSITY? PICNIC? EVENT? SCHOOL? TUNED UP COMMUNE? LEARNING SITUATION? HOME BEACH ITS A

ITS A ITS A ITS A VILLAGE TOWN CITY

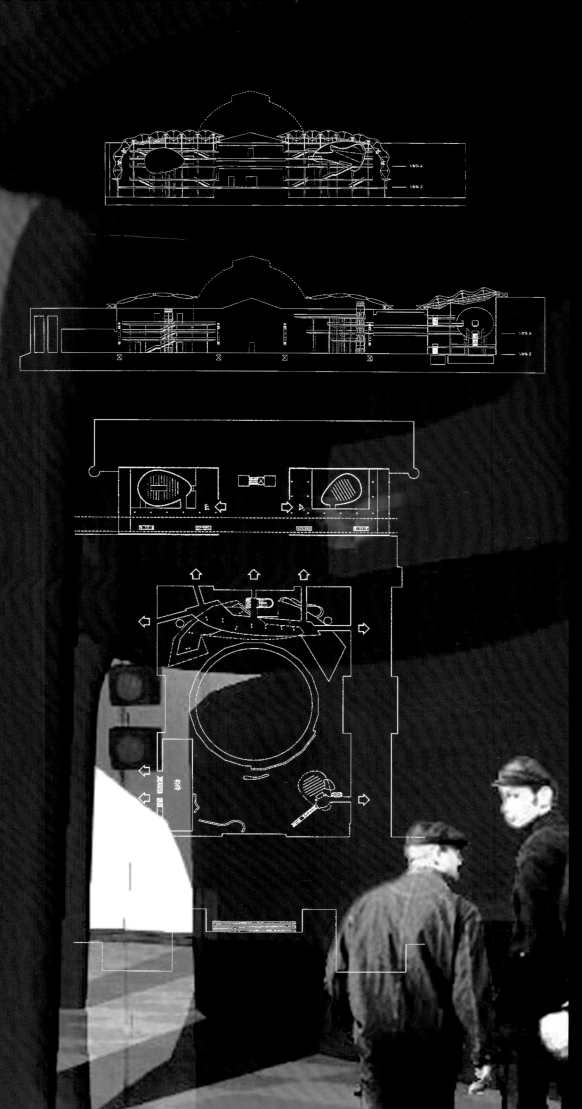

BRITISH MUSEUM COMPETITION

This year [1994] we were one of fifteen architectural practices invited to submit ideas for the British Museum competition. The brief focused on the existing library, which will lose its traditional function when the new British Library in Euston Road is complete. The basic idea was to open up the reading room to visitors and possibly demolish the surrounding bookstacks to recreate the courtyard that existed in Smirke's original scheme. The Museum also wanted competitors to look at ways of adding an education centre, temporary exhibition spaces and a more elaborate sales centre, while rationalising the connections to the existing galleries. Our proposal, which was unsuccessful, was to draw a very thin inflatable cushion roof over the whole area, from the top of the drum of the reading room to the edge of the exposed courtyard. This maintained the purity of the space and created a grand public hall, from which visitors could disperse via lifts and escalators into the various galleries. The grand hall contained a number of freestanding elements. The retail area was housed in an object like a small department store which could be open at the sides because it was covered by the main roof. The temporary exhibition area was stacked on a number of levels behind this, so that it became another object. A third object was the small cinema, which ran a short introductory video describing the exhibitions or the history of the museum. Also within the grand hall was a large reception area with a video board that talked about the events and other things of interest that day. The education centre was housed to the north of the main courtyard, in two small courtyards that we proposed to roof over with a fabric structure and take floor plates across from an independent steel structure.

In this proposal, which we did not have time to develop fully, I liked the idea of the simple gesture; an air-supported roof that allowed the facades of the courtyard to be exposed to the public gaze for the first time in a hundred years. It would have given the grand hall the sort of presence that I think a museum needs, accentuated by light and shiny steel-framed objects that represent the technology and the architecture of today.

ARTICULATIONS

lifting moving. *Hold Raise* *instant city components. Feb. 69.*

RON HERRON'S DESIGNING IS PUT TOGETHER out of separate pieces, which have to be joined together to make the whole. In ancient architectural discourse that was 'com-position' or the putting together of the volumes out of which the building was, unavoidably, 'com-posed'. The manner in which the volumes were joined together was, in a sense, negative – it was done by the wall which filled the space between one volume and the next, and the only critical point was the management of the hole in the wall by which the two volumes were topologically connected and, apart from the door-case, that was an even more negative affair.

That's a rather different piece of design business from providing for the docking of a space-ship or the plugging of a modem cable into the back of a personal computer, and the jointures and articulations of Ron Herron's designs are more in that line than they are in the line of the *poches* of the Beaux-Arts tradition. He thinks in components more than he thinks in volumes; it is in the nature of components that they have to be mated up to other components, and that means that with every component come one or more joints. And beyond a very low-technology base-line of nails or glue, any joint is something that has to be designed into the component as an integral part of it, frequently as important as the component itself.

Of course, the mode of jointure may be entirely conventional ('Stop designing nuts and bolts', Bruce Archer used to yell at his students at the Central School, 'they're all in the book already!') or they may be hidden, or they may be an overt part of the originality of the design, a manoeuvre in the strategy of conceiving it. Ron Herron's joints come in almost as many different flavours as his designs. In his sketches for buildings, they are usually no more than indicated, not detailed; they are to be presumed as conventional as the components themselves usually seem to be. But in much of his product design the joints become a kind of rhetoric, because quite often they have to indicate the use and operation of the product.

Robo-Arm / movement.
June 84

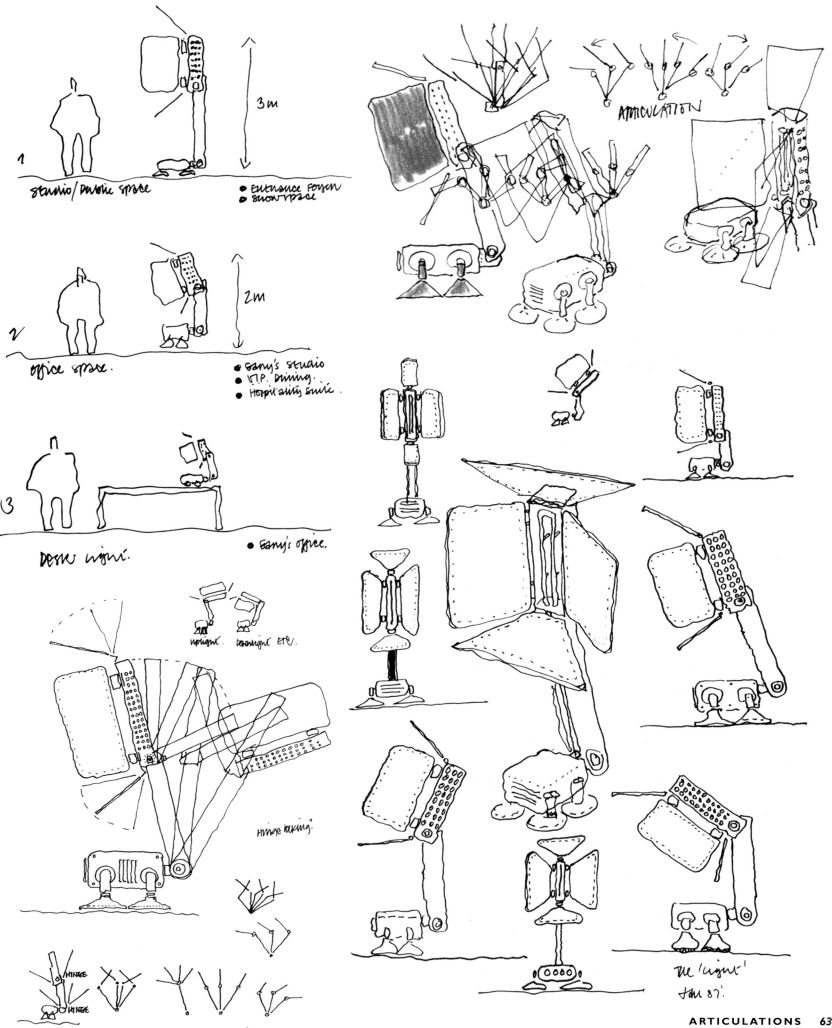

1 studio/public space
• entrance foyer
• show space

2 office space.
• Eany's studio
• VIP. Dining.
• Hospitality suite

3 desk light.
• Eany's office.

uplight   downlight ETC.

Hinge locking.

HINGE
HINGE

ARTICULATION

The 'light'
Jan 87.

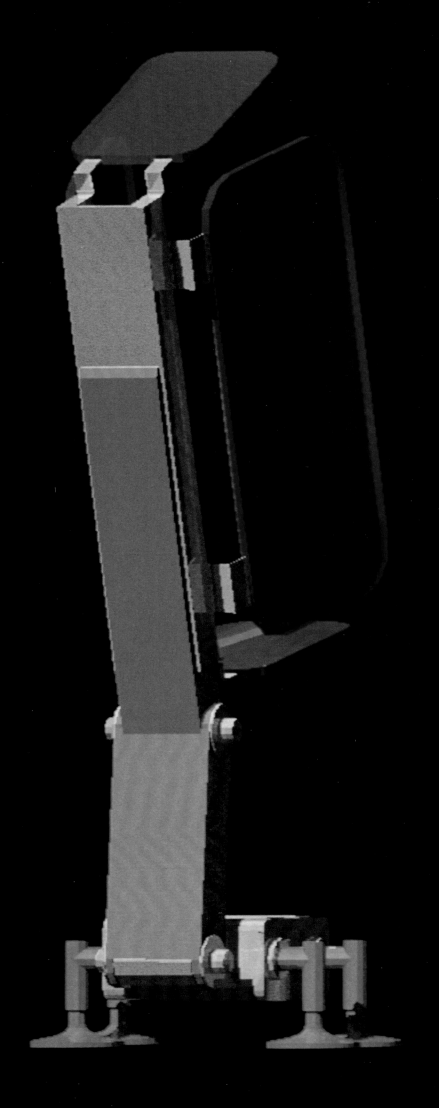

Such rhetorics do exist in regular architecture, of course – rustication on the exposed face of masonry is a negative reminder of the demands of accurate jointing on the faces that are not exposed – and they have re-appeared in the articulation of tubular constructions in much High-Tech architecture, notably that of Richard Rogers and Michael Hopkins. But in Ron Herron's product design they become a 'rhetoric of articulation' in a different sense; that of relative movements, like the adjustability of a lamp, or the grasp of the jaws of a robot arm.

Could this more rhetorical response be because he is working beyond the frontiers of his training and formation as an architect? Product design is a field where joints and articulations mean something more demanding, and something very different from what they mean in the static structures of architecture (architects don't even design hinges normally, Voysey honourably excepted). Or is it just that old fascination with toy robots, whose articulations are often very like those that Herron sketches – a fascination that is, for so many of his generation, part and parcel of being comfortable with a world of technologies, and a step (however Godzilla-Gonzo-Grotesque) on the way to coming at the essence of technology as art, rather than mere instrumentality.

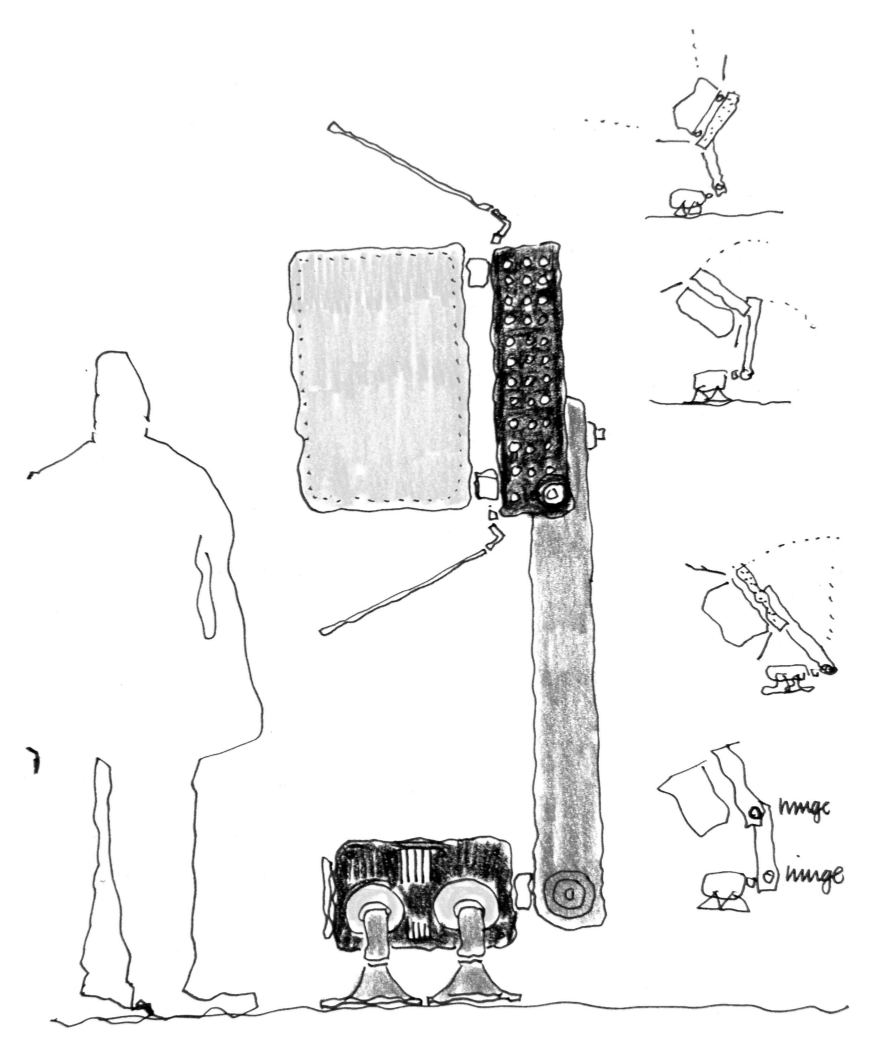

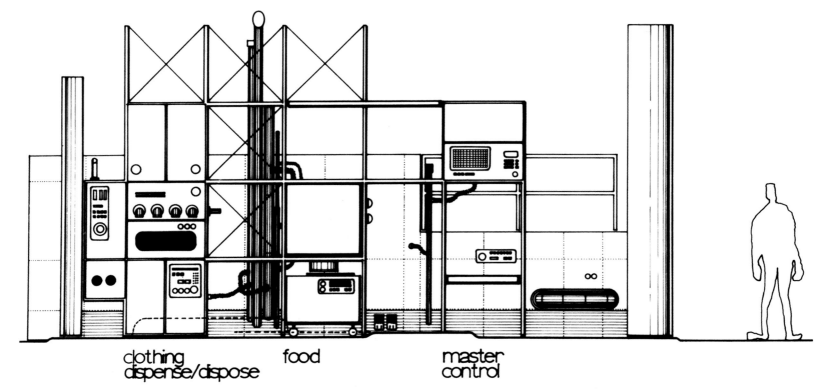

clothing
dispense/dispose

food

master
control

WEEKEND TELEGRAPH 1990   SERVICE / APPLIANCE CAGE
jan 1967

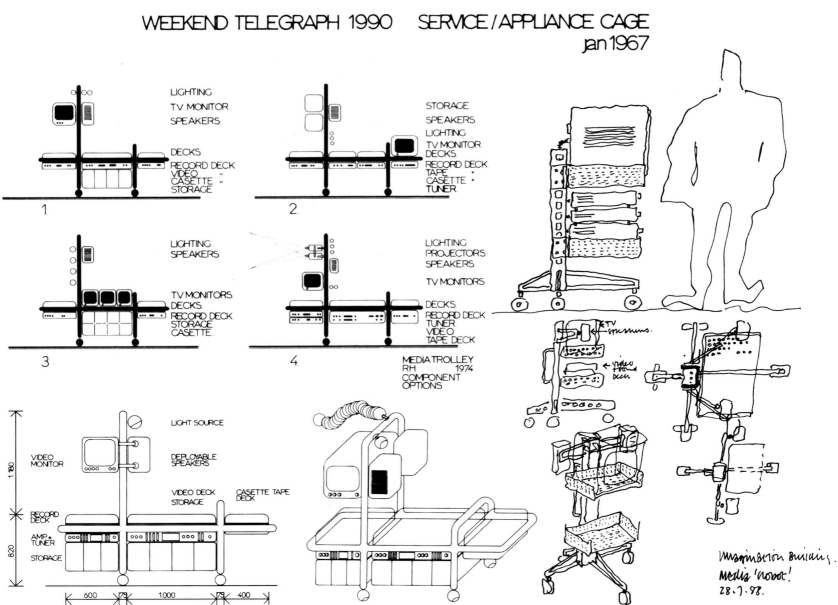

LIGHTING
T.V. MONITOR
SPEAKERS

DECKS
RECORD DECK
VIDEO   "
CASETTE   "
STORAGE

1

STORAGE
SPEAKERS
LIGHTING
TV MONITOR
DECKS
RECORD DECK
TAPE
CASETTE :
TUNER

2

LIGHTING
SPEAKERS

TV MONITORS.
DECKS
RECORD DECK
STORAGE
CASETTE.

3

LIGHTING
PROJECTORS.
SPEAKERS.

TV MONITORS

DECKS.
RECORD DECK
TUNER
VIDEO
TAPE DECK

4

MEDIA TROLLEY
RH   1974
COMPONENT
OPTIONS

1180

VIDEO
MONITOR

LIGHT SOURCE

DEPLOYABLE
SPEAKERS

VIDEO DECK   CASETTE TAPE
STORAGE   DECK

RECORD
DECK

AMP +
TUNER

820

STORAGE

600   75   1000   75   400

Imagination Building.
Media 'robot!
28.7.88.

68

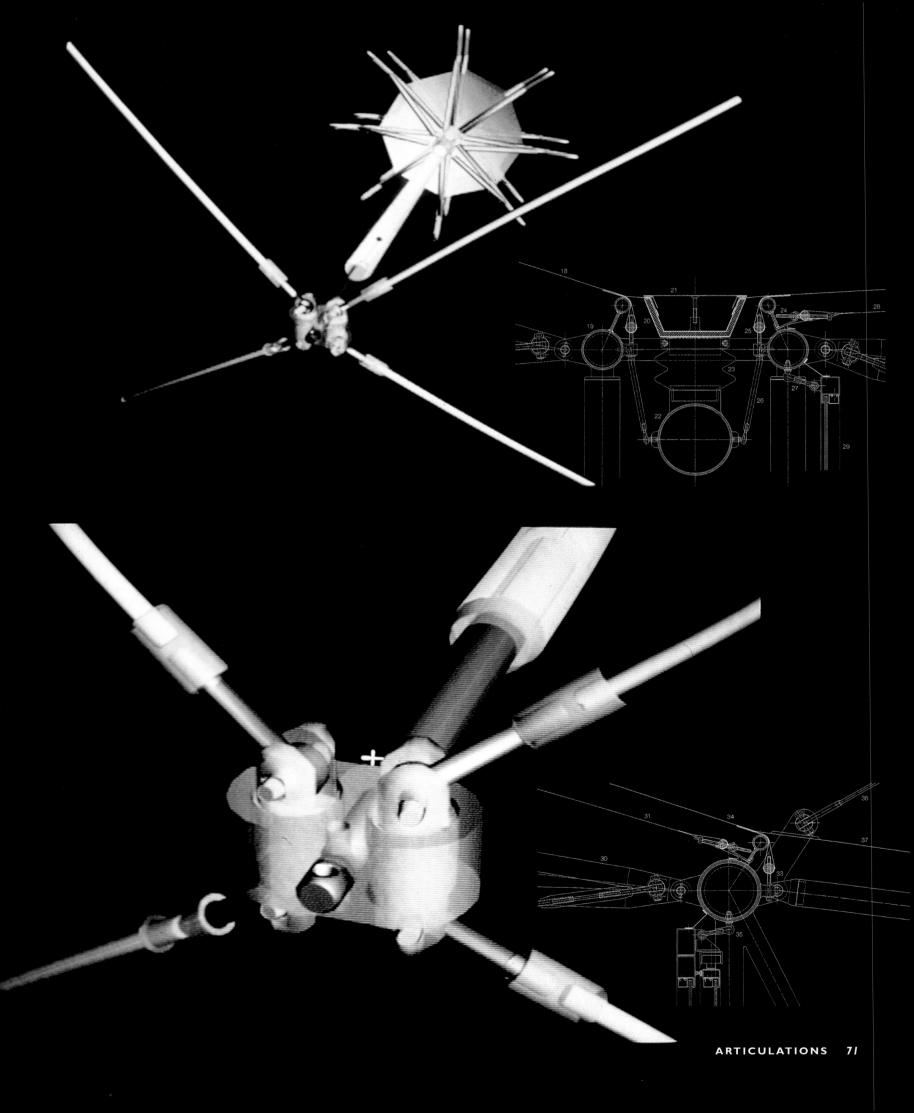

CITIES WALKING

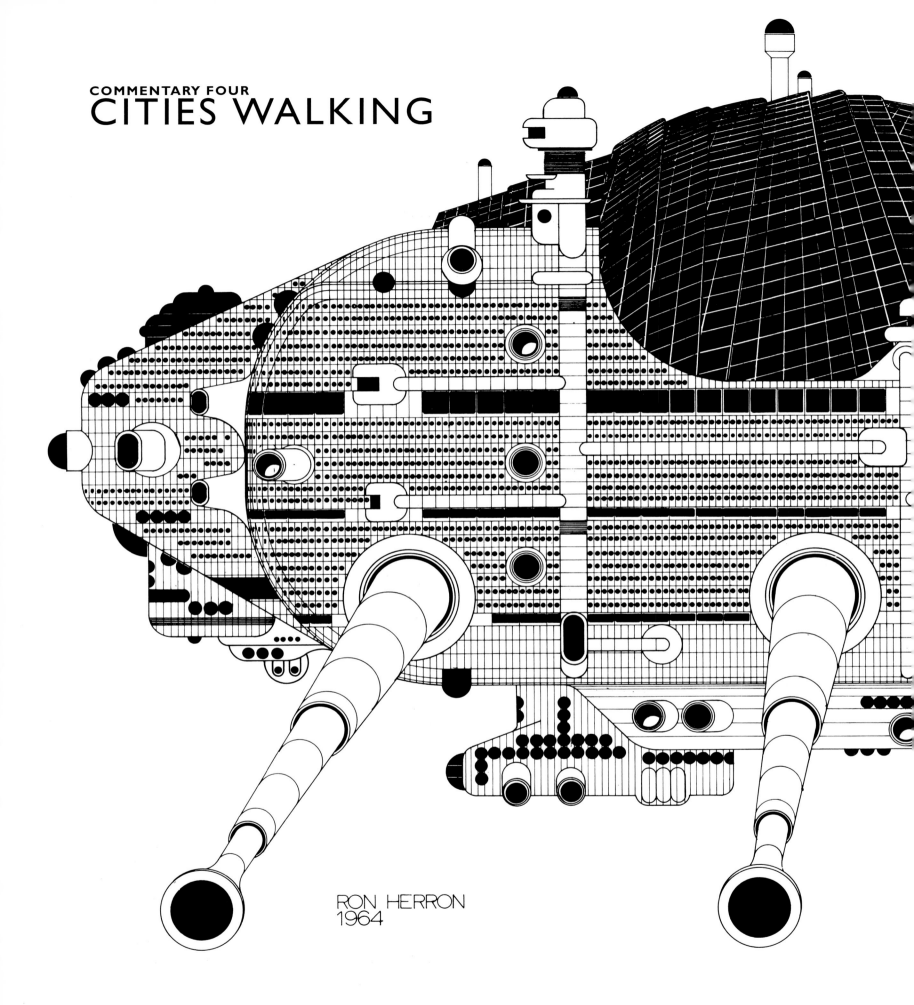

RON HERRON
1964

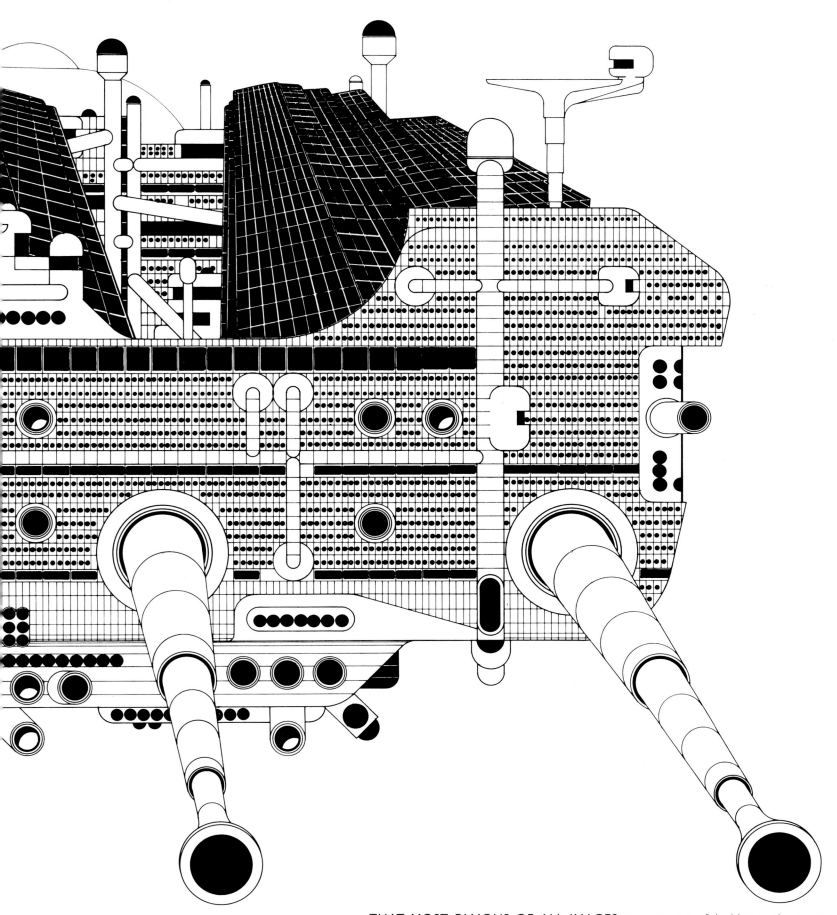

THAT MOST FAMOUS OF ALL IMAGES to come out of Archigram, the most frequently reproduced and the longest-lived, the canonical version of 'Cities Walking', is seen in flat elevation. There are other versions, invading New York and so forth, but it is that true elevation which has proven so reproducible and long-lived, finding its way

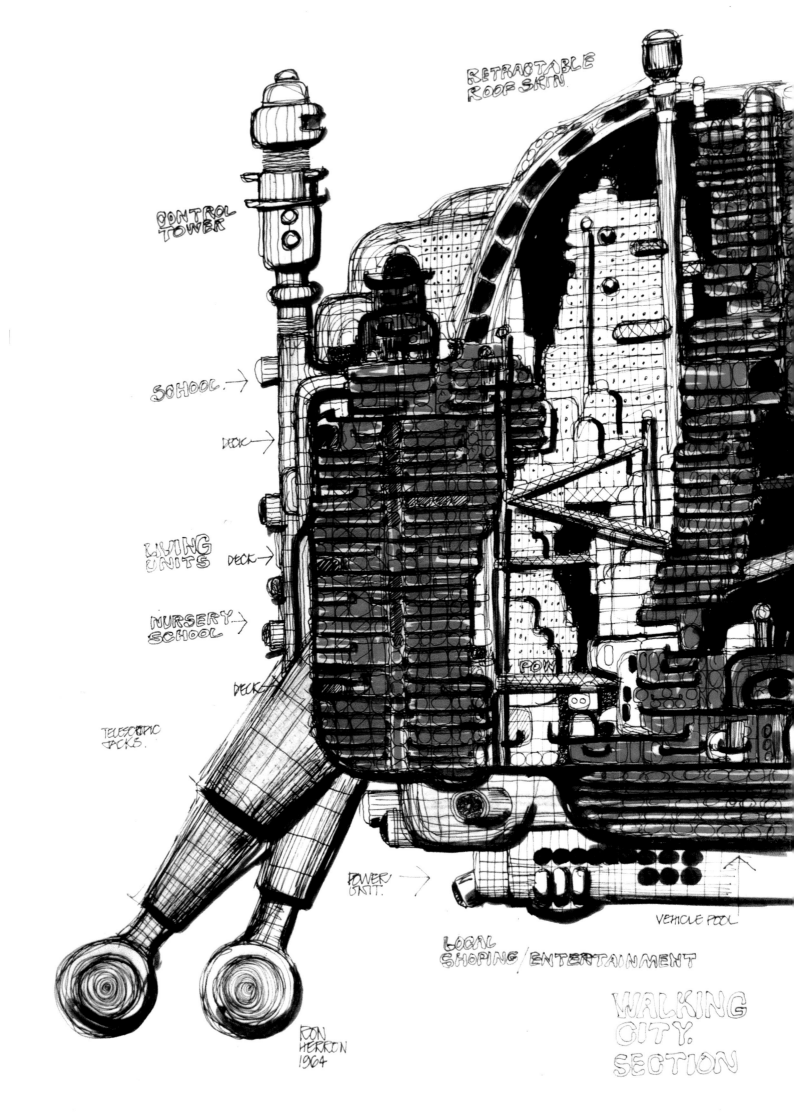

RETRACTABLE
ROOF SKIN.

CONTROL
TOWER

SCHOOL. →

DECK →

LIVING
UNITS

DECK →

NURSERY →
SCHOOL →

DECK →

TELESCOPIC
JACKS.

POWER →
UNIT.

VEHICLE POOL

LOCAL
SHOPING/ENTERTAINMENT

RON
HERRON
1964

WALKING
CITY.
SECTION

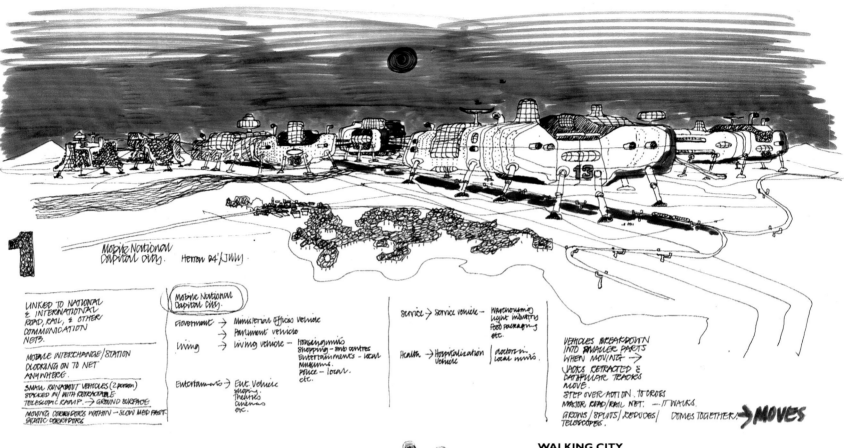

1 Mobile National Capital City. Herron 84'/July.

LINKED TO NATIONAL
& INTERNATIONAL
ROAD, RAIL, & OTHER
COMMUNICATION
NETS.

MOBILE INTERCHANGE/STATION
CLOCKING ON TO NET
ANYWHERE.

SMALL ROUNDABOUT VEHICLES (2 person)
STOCKED IN WITH RETRACTABLE
TELESCOPIC RAMP. → GROUND SURFACE.

MOVING CORRIDORS WITHIN – SLOW MED FAST
STATIC CORRIDORS

Mobile National
Capital City.

Government → Ministerial Offices Vehicle
→ Parliament vehicle

Living → Living vehicle → Housing/units
Shopping – snb centres
Entertainments – local
Museums.
Police – local.
etc.

Entertainments → Ent. Vehicle
Shopping
Theatres
Cinemas
etc.

Service → Service vehicle – Warehousing
Light industry
Food packaging
etc.

Health → Hospitalization
Vehicle
Doctors in
local units.

VEHICLES BREAKDOWN
INTO SMALLER PARTS
WHEN MOVING →
JACKS RETRACTED &
CATAPILLAR TRACKS
MOVE.
STEP OVER/ACTION . TO CROSS
MAJOR ROAD/RAIL NET. – IT WALKS.
GROWS/SPLITS/REDUCES/ DOMES TOGETHER: → MOVES
TELESCOPES.

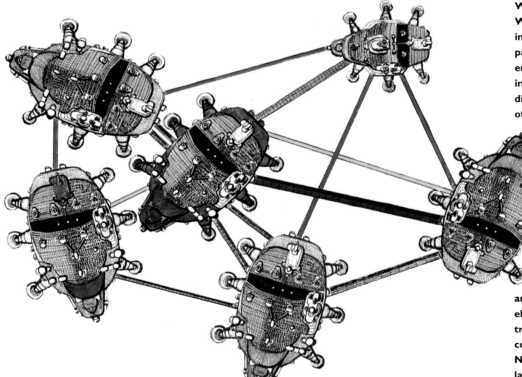

into most of the histories or commentaries on Modernism that take any notice of visionary design.

One testimony to its power as an image was its use on the poster and catalogue cover for the heavy-metal show of modern architectural drawings, *VISION DER MODERNE*, at the German Architecture Museum in Frankfurt in 1986. The other important one is that major-league pundits like Sigfried Giedion, the architectural historian, and Constantinos Doxiadis, a Greek urban theorist of great weight in the 1960s, both took it seriously enough to attack it for presenting an 'inhuman' urban vision. 'But [one said to Giedion] it's only

WALKING CITY

Walking City came out of the ideas of indeterminancy prevalent in the 1960s, particularly the idea of the city as a changing entity which could respond to the inhabitants' immediate needs. I took a slightly different direction and looked at the idea of indeterminacy of place – Walking City was the result.

The idea was of a world capital capable of being anywhere in the world at any time, a kind of United Nations City taken to an extreme. There was a whole family of these vehicles, containing all the elements you would find in a functioning city: business quarter, offices, housing, public and private services. Some had detachable auxiliary units, such as hospitals and disaster units.

The standard Walking City had extendible arms, which could connect with other walking elements, with the ground and sea, allowing the transfer of goods and materials. The original collage, which I called 'Cities Moving', was set in New York; the desert version was made much later, for the 1973 Archigram exhibition at the Institute of Contemporary Arts.

A description in the *International Times* in the late 1960s or early 1970s likened the Walking City to a war machine. The paper had made its own collage which had these vehicles crushing houses and tanks and so on. I must admit that I'd always seen it differently; as an object which moved slowly across the earth like a giant hovercraft, only using its legs as a levelling device when it settled on its site. To me, it was a rather friendly-looking machine.

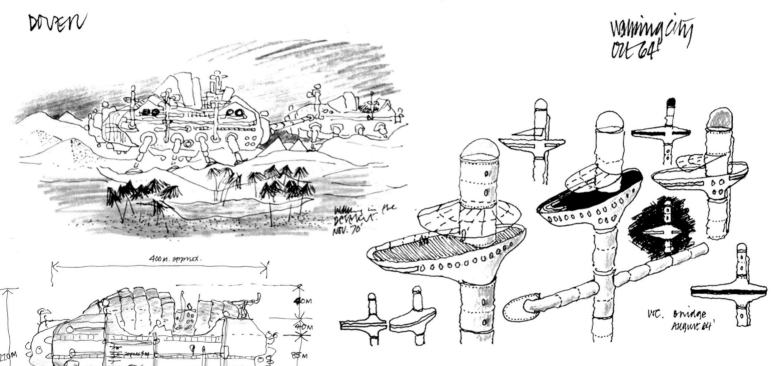

DOVER

walking city oct '64

WC. bridge August 64

a drawing! It's not that serious!' 'Who would make such elaborated a drawing if he did not want it to be taken seriously?', the earnest Swiss countered – and in a way he had a point. It is indeed 'elaborated', labour-intensively so (try counting all those windows!) and drawing is still a very serious business in architecture.

Furthermore, like all the best Archigram images, it is intensely and precisely detailed, so that even when you have worked out that the apparent geometry makes any movement of the legs impossible, your imagination can still visualise this monster, surely descended from those in *The War of the Worlds*, advancing relentlessly over land and sea, intent on its rendezvous with destiny in the East River, under the shadow of the Brooklyn Bridge. The only thing that can have made it fearsome was the proposition that it should move – after all, the period envisaged far vaster fixed projects, such as Tange's proposal to build all over Tokyo bay (of which Doxiadis apparently approved). One or two even got built, as at Cumbernauld in Scotland. Clearly, it was felt that something the size of a city centre should know its place, in the townscape, in history, and in Western culture, and not offer to amble off in the night and show up in Philadelphia in the morning.

It was the first major manifestation of the mixture of technological high-spirits, urban wit and obsessive draftsmanship that has characterised all the best work from Ron Herron's cunning hand. Its place in his *oeuvre* is assured. In the intellectual history of 20th-century architecture it seems likely to endure as a kind of landmark to a shift in sentiment, taste, *weltanschauung*, or something. Because what got crushed under the mighty feet of this stalking vision was not 'humanity' but the empty claims of the 'functionalism' that had once been the driving energy of modern architecture, but had since become a paralysing inertia in the hands of the academies and the establishments.

The old libidinous mechanical kraken of Modernism had re-awakened and raised itself from the placid waters of the dead sea of current architecture, and the panic was on. Had the panicked hung around a bit, they would also have seen that marvellous, witty and life-enhancing later drawing of four or five walking cities gathered together in friendly interlinked intercourse…

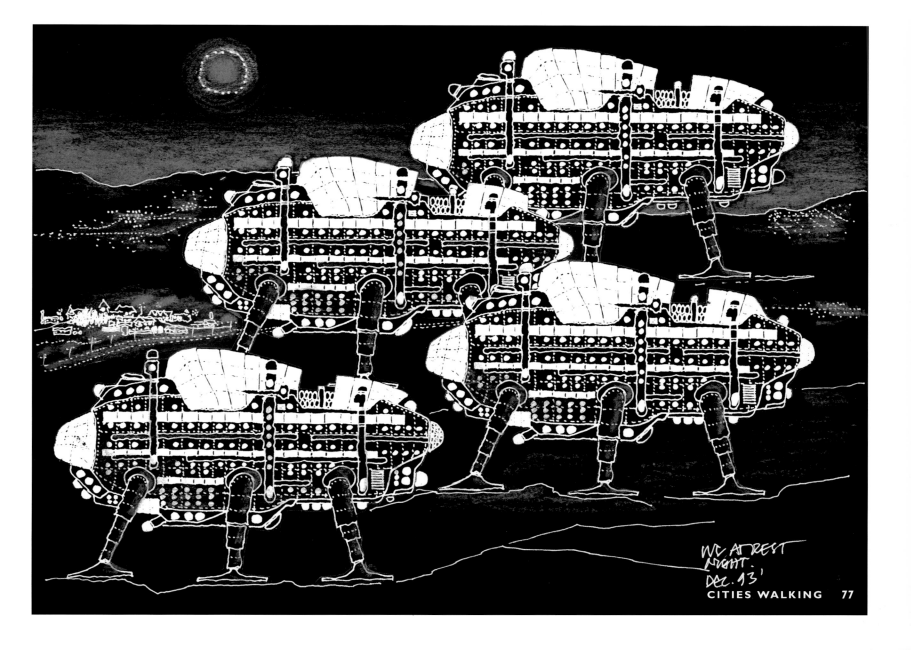

CITIES : MOVING

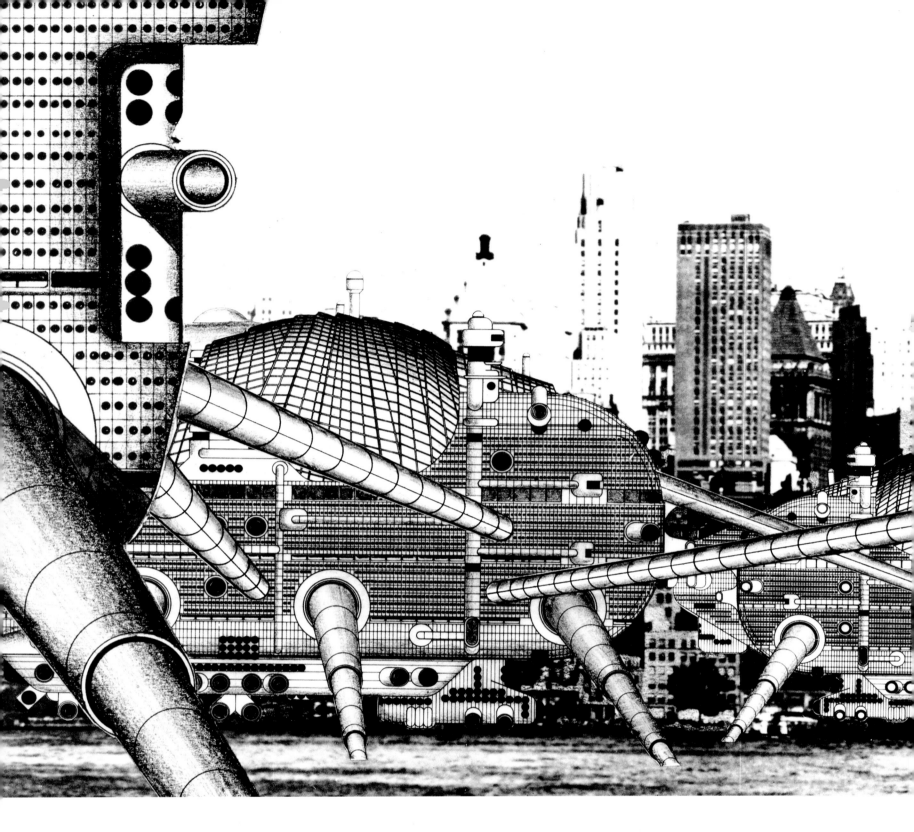

NEW YORK — WR.
July 1964

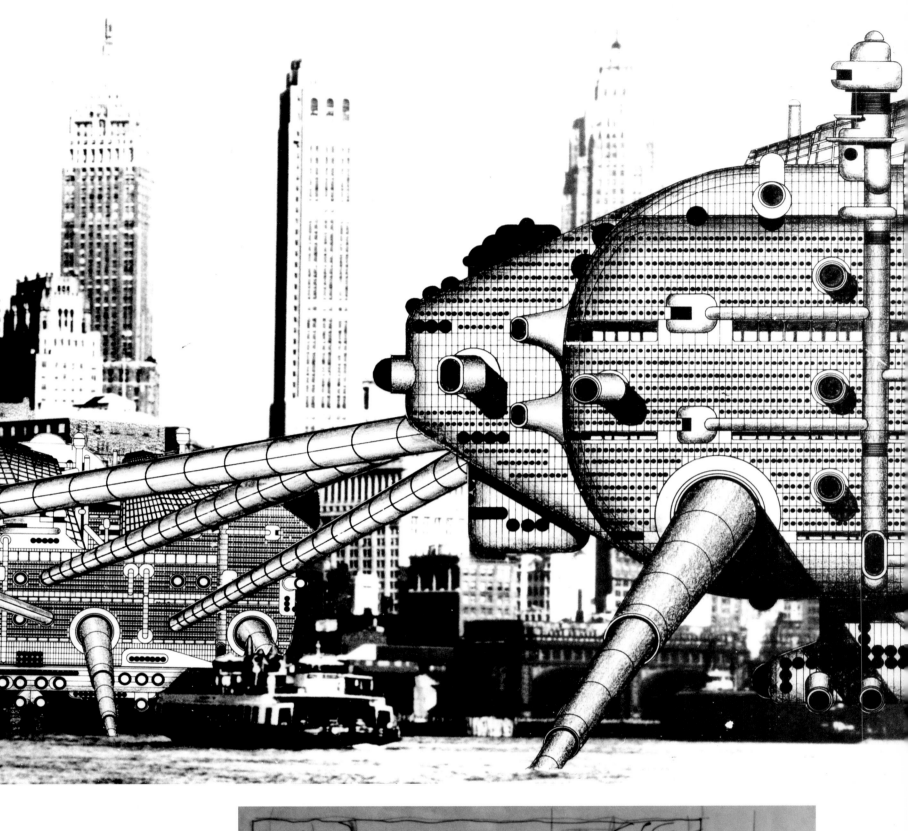

'CITIES'
MOVING

3 or 4 vehicles
montage.
SIZE. - Full Pic.
RH. Jan 1963.

SUBURBAN SETS, ROYAL PETS

OF ALL THE VISIONS OFFERED by Ron Herron over the years, one of the most persistent, most difficult to explain to non-British architects, and most difficult for British architects to accept, has been that of suburban illusionism, and its crucial corollary, palatial image-making. How can one explain, even to the Brits, that – yes – it is possible for a supposedly radical architect to accept at face value the 'Castles on the Ground' of bourgeois suburbia, and their presiding genius, the irretrievably bourgeois House of Windsor, with its polo-ponies and corgis.

With Ron Herron, the words 'face value' are crucial because he knows what is behind the architectural face, the social facade of suburbia – he lives there. In a bog-standard, by-the-book basic speculative semi-det hard by the Underground Railway. Or, rather, what you see from the street is basic semi-det, complete with a couple of Fords in the remains of a front garden; what happens round the back is – exactly as in one of his Suburban Sets projects – entirely his own affair and his family fantasy. The public facade is conventional, the secret garden is … a secret. The dichotomy is a long-established source of rage to architectural reformers to whom the destruction of suburbia ('Come friendly bombs, and fall on Slough, etc.') is the essential prerequisite of some architecturally 'better' England where everyone will inhabit high-density apartments (modern or Post-Modern) and lead their private life at cafe-tables in the public piazza.

Ultimately, the crime of suburbia is to confuse that difference between

'city' and 'country' on which the values of so much British culture were based, even before Raymond Williams wrote the book that made them Holy Writ. And what cannot but divert close observers of both architecture and Ron Herron is that he is – in so many ways – on the same side as the reformers, since one valid (but neither exclusive nor exhaustive) reading of his Suburban Sets is the undermining of suburbia from within and by its own implicit value system.

The inner contradiction that will destroy suburbia-as-we-know-it has nothing to do with Marxist theory and a great deal to do with, e.g., picture windows. Architects – other than Ron Herron – seem to believe that the function of picture-windows is to see out; suburbanites (and Ron Herron) know, contrariwise, that the function of picture-windows is *to be seen*. By the neighbours. That is why picture-windows have to be on the front of the house, where people can see them, even if the view they might command is at the back or the side.

'If you've got it, why not flaunt it', says the wisdom of two Fords in every front garden. And there is the true contradiction that adds piquancy to Ron Herron's suburban vision. All those backyard secrets, all that illusionistic gismology, all those gazebos and grounded 747s, floodlit fountains and electronic tomatoes must, sooner or later, come bursting through the facade into public view… and their flaunting will blow the cover of all the latter-day Mr Pooters (who may include a Mr Herron) who thought that you could have your secret and eat it, so to speak.

PERSONALISED WINDOW SETS FOR INCLUSION
IN PUBLIC SET FACADE.   YOUR PUBLIC FACE..............LIFE-STYLE DREAM.
ALL WINDOW SETS INCLUDE INTEGRAL BACKLIGHTING.
OPTIONAL DRAPES OR BLINDS
COLOR PHOTO BASE TO SET GUARANTEED NOT TO FADE.......................

SS·C·W1

SS·C·W2

SS·C·W3

SS·C·W4

SS·C·W5

SS·C·W6

WINDOW SETS.

SUBURBAN SETS
COMPONENTS
AUG.74' ●NTS. 189:101

It is a fair bet that Herron's perception of these dilemmas, and his manifest enjoyment of them, were brought to a sharp edge by his years in Los Angeles, notoriously the city of (to mangle the proverb) Six Illusions in Search of a Suburb. But he is quite right to focus his vision on London, and on London's ultimate suburban housewife, Elizabeth II, who seems to represent the condition to which all suburban housewifery aspires. And long before the media cottoned on to what was happening, Ron Herron had clearly divined that QE2, and her extended family of princelings and princely wifelings, are a self-promoting, self-actuating, continuous, never-off-your-screens media event, to whom all buildings and places, even Buckingham Palace and Westminster Abbey, are simply permanent sound-stages. In this world of palatial image-manipulating, the Royal Sets of Ron Herron are fair comment as well as *lèse-majesté*, and quite as good as the real thing because they *are* the real thing. Just as the illusions in the backyards of suburbia are almost as good as the reality of frontyard suburbia because they are – on the point of becoming – the real thing.

MONTE CARLO

The two Monte Carlo projects were both competition projects made in the early 1970s. The first, Features Monte Carlo, was one that Archigram won. My involvement in the project was limited by the fact that I was living in Los Angeles at the time: ideas were exchanged by post with London. I made a proposal which had to do with an adjustable cage that would accept all the elements of the entertainment place, a mix of conference, banqueting and sports facilities. The cage sat on one of the few open spaces in the Principality, a piece of land that jutted out into the sea. I was interested in pursuing the Instant City idea and using the cage to spill out the elements that would make up these changing facilities.

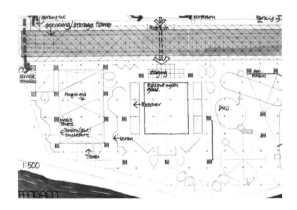

In the meantime, back in London, the decision had been made to go underground with the events space, which was a rather nice idea as it preserved the park, the only open space in the area. I then contributed some sketches towards the scheme, showing the ever-changing space inside and the naked parts that facilitated the change. But probably the only drawing I made that was ultimately used was for what we called the 'Stick Plug'. This was a little element like a parking meter, or flag over a golf hole, that allowed people in the park over the building to plug into a grid and tune in to the events below. It transmitted sound. There was no video at the time, although if there had been, I'm sure I'd have used it. The Stick Plug also provided cool air, air to blow up your lilo, and even suntan lotion.

What's interesting is that while I was doing this David Greene was working on something similar, and although the objects turned out different the facility was the same in both

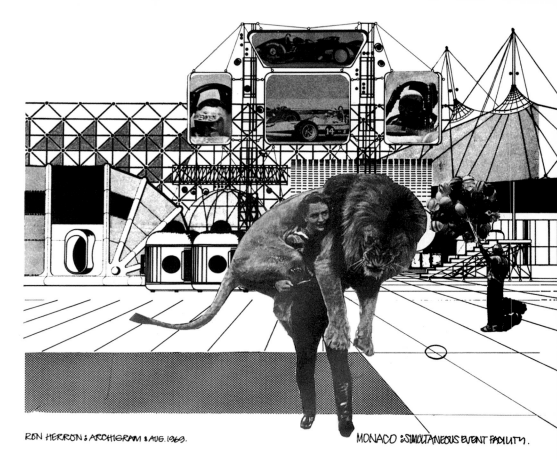

RON HERRON & ARCHIGRAM & AUG. 1969.   MONACO : SIMULTANEOUS EVENT FACILITY.

cases. This happened quite often during that Archigram period. One of the group would be working through an idea when a letter describing a project on the same tack would pop up out of the blue from another one of us somewhere in the States or in England. A similar way of thinking emerged in different forms, obviously depending on the individual. During our work on the Features Monte Carlo project, we were invited to present competition ideas for a Summer Casino, a nightclub cum gala space (right). Archigram came up with two different versions, one that Peter ran with, another that I ran with. These two things were going on the same site and they had the same brief but each showed quite a different hand. These were exciting times in the Archigram office, with great competition.

THE SETS PROJECTS

The Sets projects started in the early 1970s with an element from the programme for the Monte Carlo Casino, a very theatrical outdoor space for events like the annual Red Cross gala ball. Our idea was to make an architecture which serviced the space and covered it in the event of rain, but at the same time was continually transformed by movie-sets. So the space could be Elizabethan, or Modern, or Art Deco, or whatever suited the event, as was illustrated in a series of collages at the time. The notion of the Suburban Sets came from talking to my son Andrew, who was then at school and writing a paper about the architecture of Suburbia. We invented a suburb based on Woodford, where we live. The architecture was paper-thin scenery reflecting the public face which people chose to present to others. The facade windows served as Sets: the design and decoration would change according to what the occupants wanted the outside world to believe about their life-styles. Most importantly, there was behind the Sets a private world, a place where people could make their own environments. We chose three families to illustrate the idea: an architect who could use the notion intelligently, a camping enthusiast who had a trailer home behind his facade (a really high-living camper), and a former bomber pilot whose private Set was the fuselage of an old B-24 Liberator. The idea was that they could choose the environment that they wanted to live in – they could be in Hawaii, or India, or on a bombing mission. From my observation, this is exactly what happens in the suburb: people build their own myth and reality into their houses.

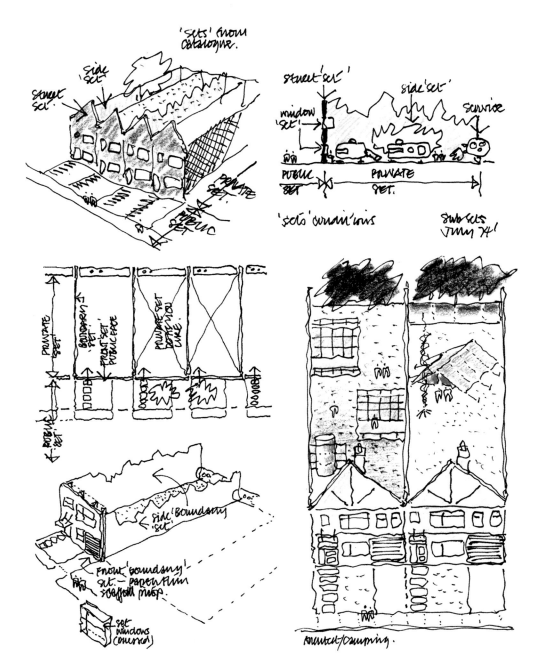

SUBURBAN SETS

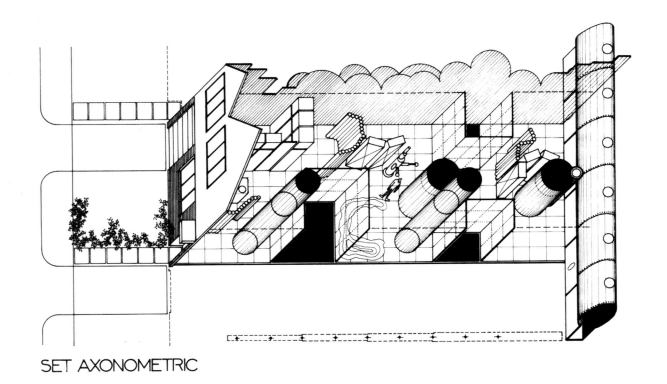

SET AXONOMETRIC

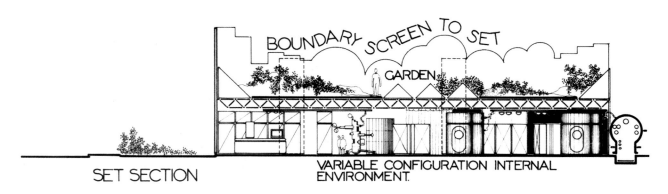

BOUNDARY SCREEN TO SET

GARDEN

SET SECTION

VARIABLE CONFIGURATION INTERNAL ENVIRONMENT.

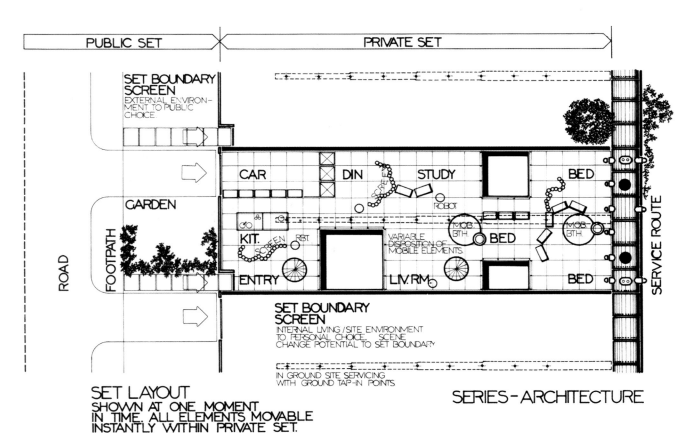

PUBLIC SET	PRIVATE SET

SET BOUNDARY SCREEN
EXTERNAL ENVIRON-MENT TO PUBLIC CHOICE.

ROAD

FOOTPATH

GARDEN

CAR   DIN   STUDY   BED

KIT.   MOB BTH.   BED   MOB BTH.

VARIABLE DISPOSITION OF MOBILE ELEMENTS

ENTRY   LIV. RM.   BED

SCREEN   RBT.   ROBOT

SERVICE ROUTE

SET BOUNDARY SCREEN
INTERNAL LIVING/SITE ENVIRONMENT TO PERSONAL CHOICE. SCENE CHANGE POTENTIAL TO SET BOUNDARY.

IN GROUND SITE SERVICING WITH GROUND TAP-IN POINTS

SET LAYOUT
SHOWN AT ONE MOMENT IN TIME. ALL ELEMENTS MOVABLE INSTANTLY WITHIN PRIVATE SET.

SERIES-ARCHITECTURE

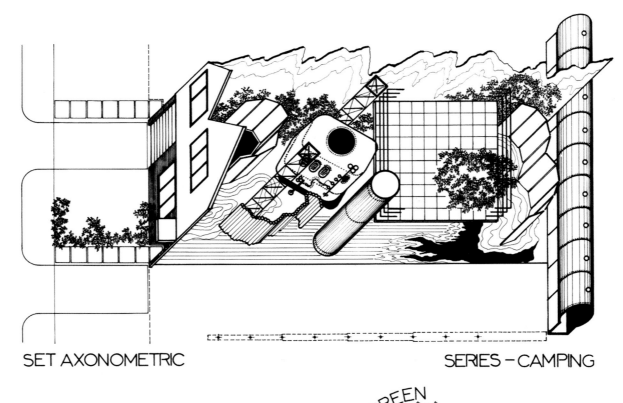

SET AXONOMETRIC   SERIES – CAMPING

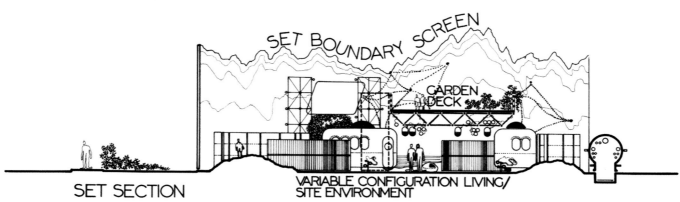

SET BOUNDARY SCREEN

GARDEN DECK

SET SECTION

VARIABLE CONFIGURATION LIVING/
SITE ENVIRONMENT

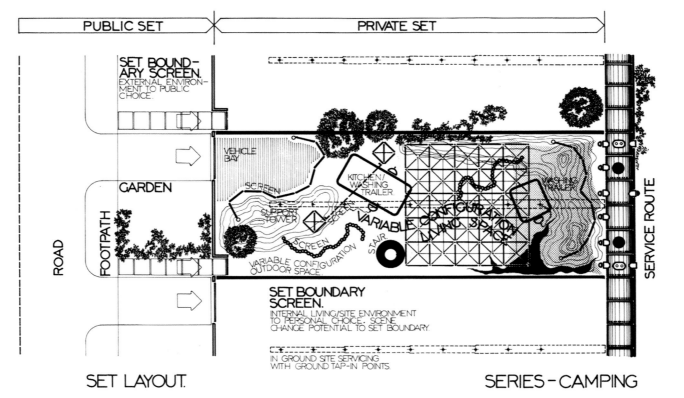

PUBLIC SET   PRIVATE SET

SET BOUND-
ARY SCREEN.
EXTERNAL ENVIRON-
MENT TO PUBLIC
CHOICE.

VEHICLE
BAY

GARDEN

ROAD

FOOTPATH

SCREEN

KITCHEN/
WASHING
TRAILER

WASTE
WATER

SUPPORT
TOWER

SCREEN

VARIABLE CONFIGURA-
TION LIVING SPACE

SERVICE ROUTE

SCREEN

STAIR

VARIABLE CONFIGURATION
OUTDOOR SPACE.

SET BOUNDARY
SCREEN.
INTERNAL LIVING/SITE ENVIRONMENT
TO PERSONAL CHOICE. SCENE
CHANGE POTENTIAL TO SET BOUNDARY.

IN GROUND SITE SERVICING
WITH GROUND TAP-IN POINTS.

SET LAYOUT.   SERIES – CAMPING

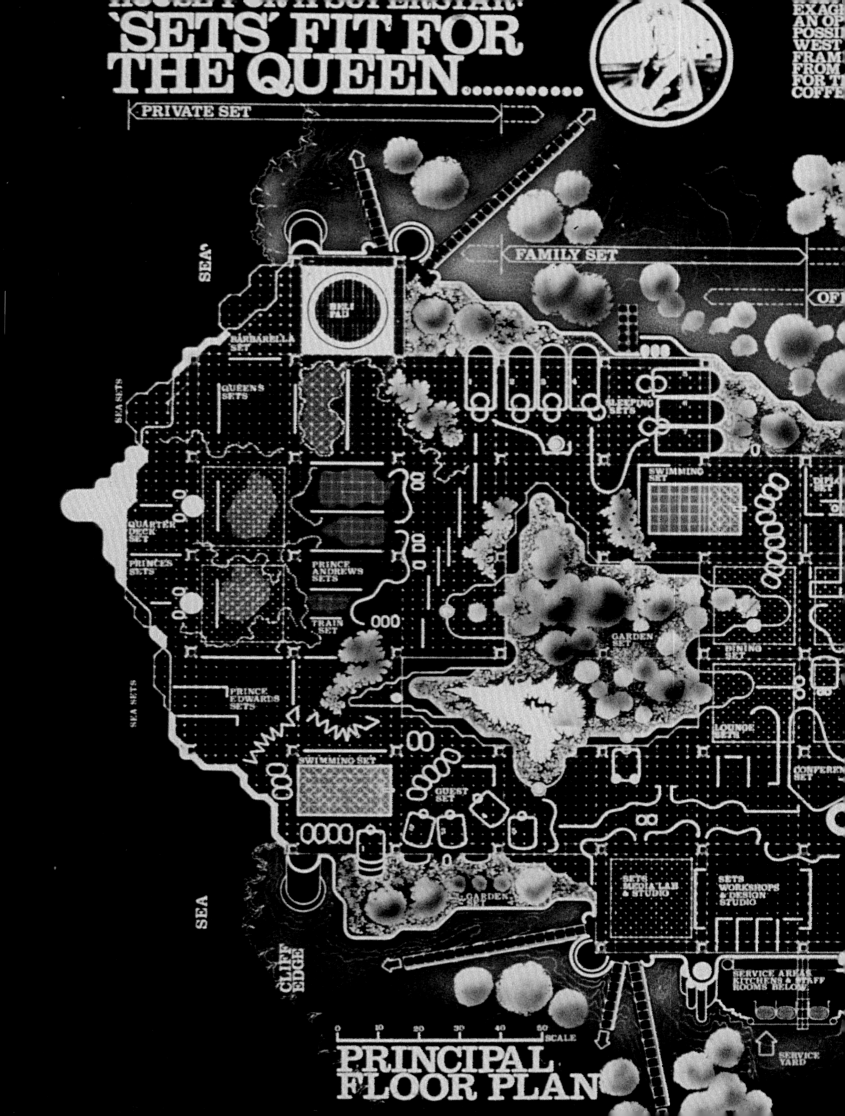

'SETS' FIT FOR
THE QUEEN...........

PRINCIPAL
FLOOR PLAN

90

FOR THE QUEEN.............. THE QUEEN WAS CHOSEN AS ONE WHO HAS AN PUBLIC TO PRIVATE LIFESTYLE. THIS INTERESTED ME IN THAT IT GAVE NARIO THROUGH WHICH I COULD PHANTASISE. PARTICULARLY ABOUT THE TINGS. THE DRAWINGS SHOW A 'RETREAT' ON A REMOTE SECTION OF THE OF SCOTLAND. USING THE MOVIE/STAGE SET ANALOGY, THE RETREAT IS A WITHIN WHICH 'SETS' CAN BE CONSTRUCTED AT WILL, AND CHANGED DAY, WEEK TO WEEK, MONTH TO MONTH............... 'CALL UP A NEW SET' T WING PHILIP. I'M FED-UP WITH ROYAL ROCOCO. LET'S TRY A FIFTIES SET............................

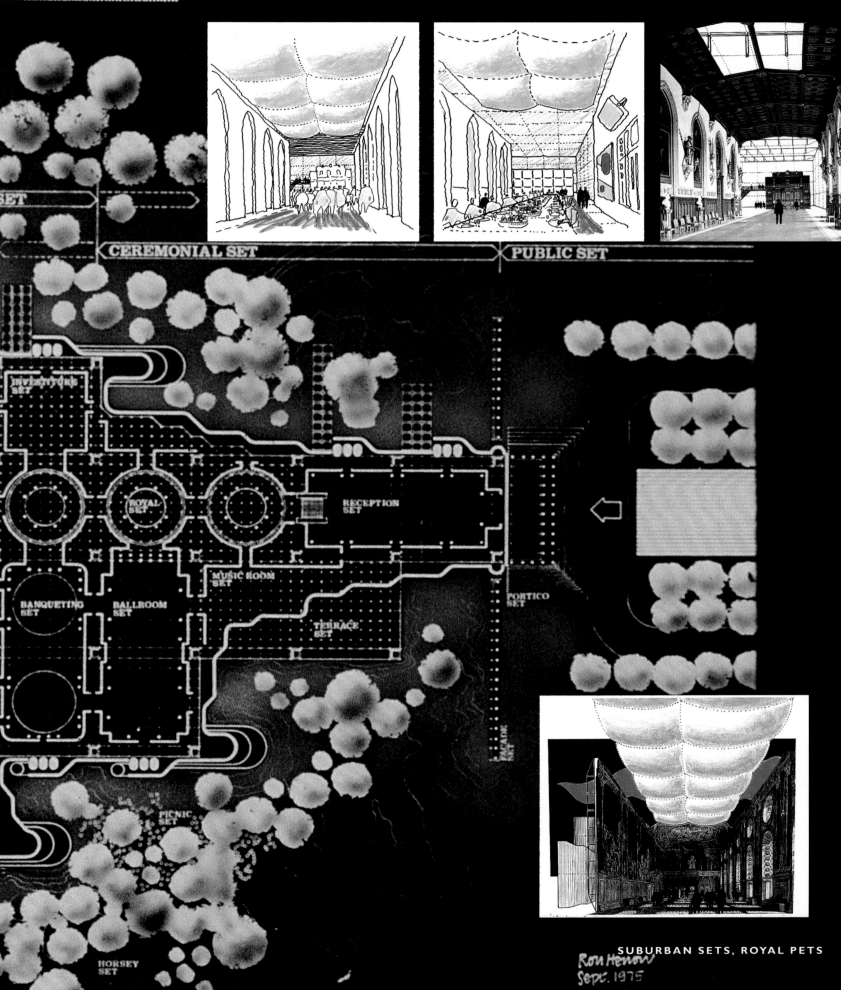

CEREMONIAL SET

PUBLIC SET

INVESTITURE SET

ROYAL SET

RECEPTION SET

MUSIC ROOM SET

BANQUETING SET

BALLROOM SET

TERRACE SET

PORTICO SET

FACADE SET

PICNIC SET

HORSEY SET

Ron Herron
Sept. 1975

The 'Sets Fit for the Queen' of 1975 started off as an entry to the Shinkenchiku competition to design 'A House for a Superstar'. I chose the Queen and the Royal Family as Britain's ultimate superstars and designed a palace which had as its antecedents the studios of Paramount and the great Hollywood production companies, as well as the stage-set facades of the Regent's Park terraces and Disneyland's Main Street, USA. The premiss was that the Royal Family lived in an essentially theatrical condition, moving from one set to another depending on what role they were expected to play at the time. For state occasions they could call up any kind of setting, be it coffee bar modern or Baroque or medieval or Art Deco. They had at their fingertips a catalogue from which they could choose or invent the new settings, including private settings where they could live out their own dreams at will. A workforce of people would build and change the Sets. The building would twitch and shiver into life, becoming what the family wanted – the ultimate dream palace.

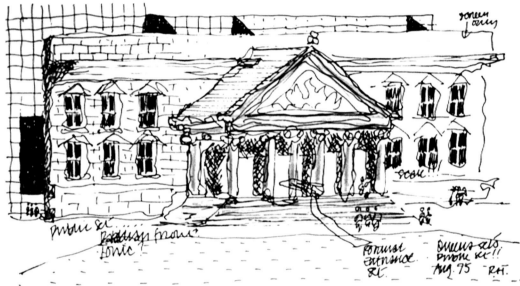

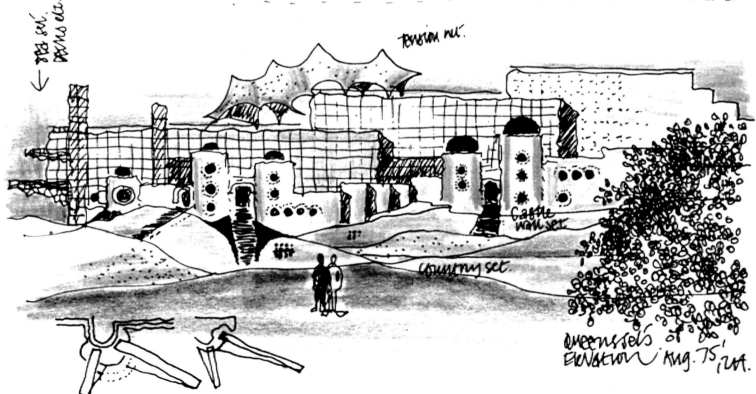

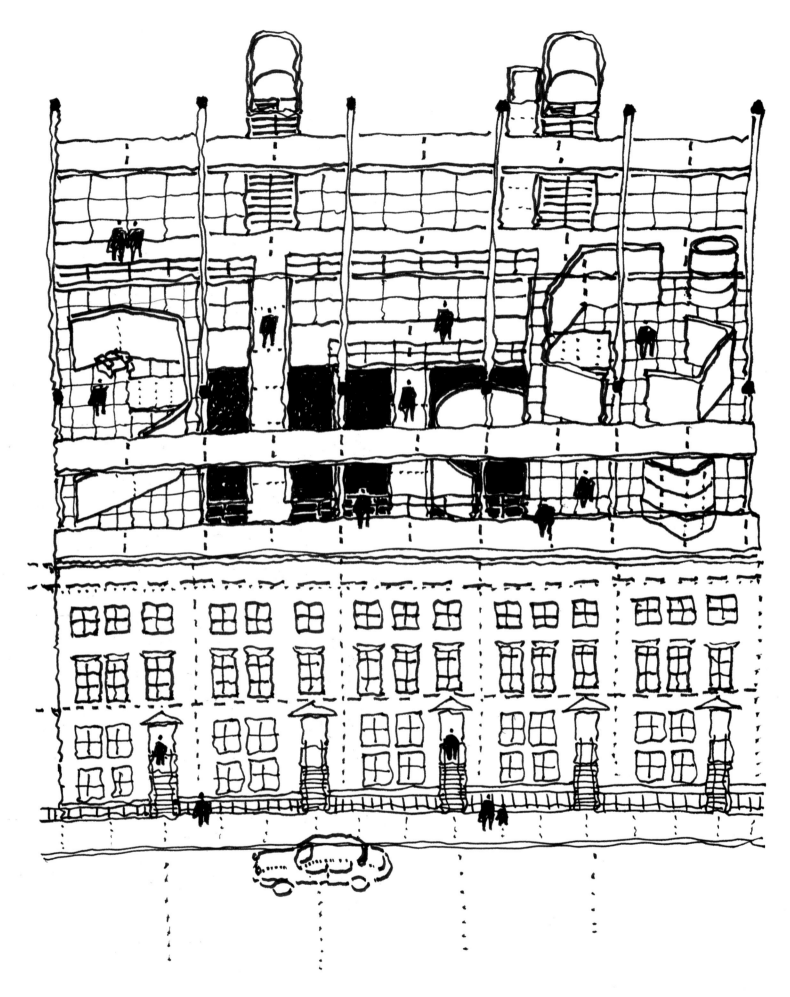

axo from street.

Garris House
19·8·90

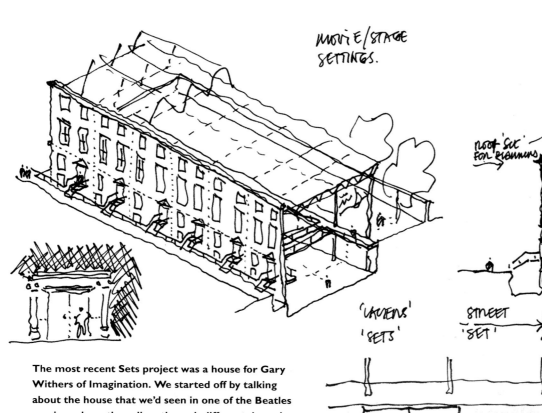

MOVIE/STAGE
SETTINGS.

ROOF 'SET' FOR RUNNERS

studio panes

'LUTIENS'
'SETS

STREET
'SET'

HOUSE
'SET'

GARDEN
'SET'

The most recent Sets project was a house for Gary Withers of Imagination. We started off by talking about the house that we'd seen in one of the Beatles movies, where they all go through different doors in a terrace and end up in a single space, a huge shed. The proposition was to buy a series of terrace houses in London, so you could enter through a number of front doors… and find yourself in a shell. The whole space would be contained by the frontage with an adaptable frame behind it to carry variable floors and an adjustable roof. Gary's house would become sets that he could change at will. A space that was a vestibule and dining room one day could be a totally different vestibule and library or living room the next. It could be dressed up in a Baroque or a Modernist manner, just as Gary wished. In other words, the Sets would be Fit for Gary.

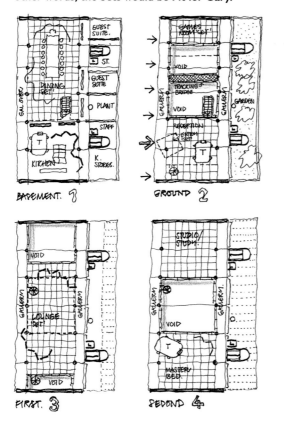

BASEMENT. 8

GROUND 2

FIRST. 3

SECOND 4

'reception/entry' set

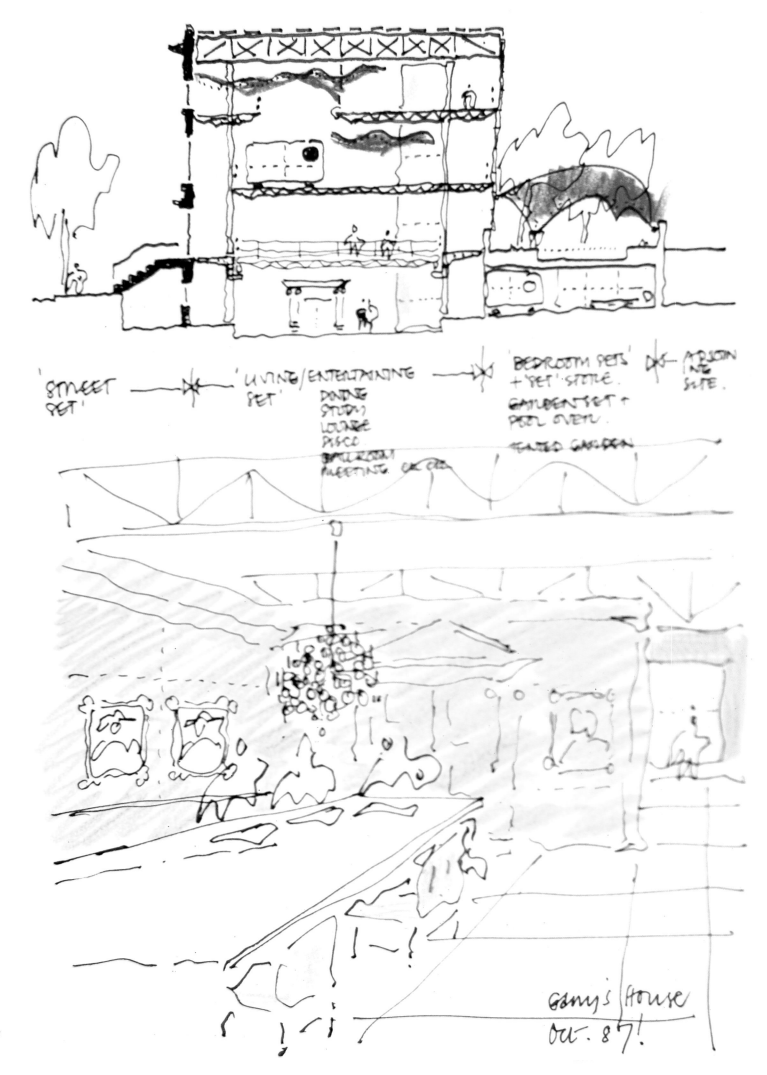

'STREET
PET'.

'LIVING/ENTERTAINING
PET'
DINING
STUDY
LOUNGE
DISCO
BILLIARD
MEETING CR CR

'BEDROOM PETS'
+ 'PET' STABLE.
GARDEN PET +
POOL OVER.

TENTED GARDEN.

A'BJOIN
ING
SITE.

Gany's House
Oct. 87!

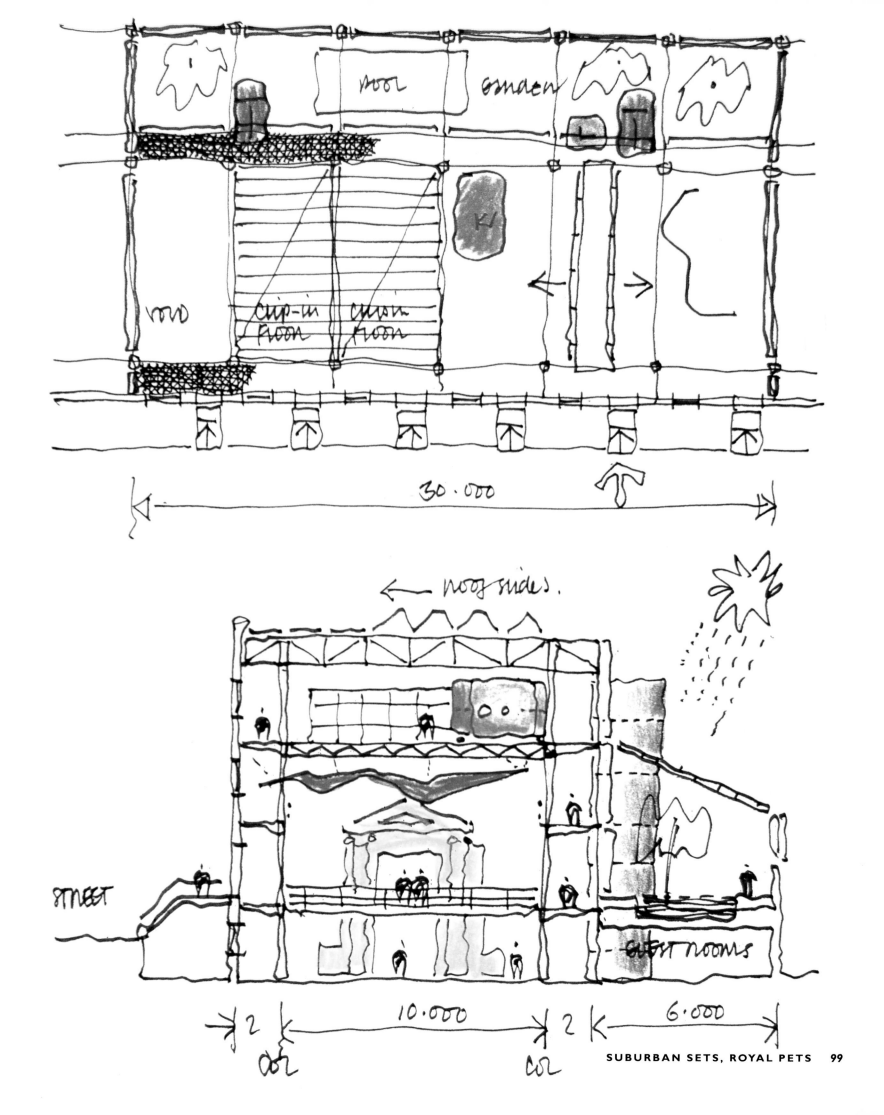

pool   garden

void   clip-in   custom
        floor   floor

K/

30.000

roof slides.

STREET

GUEST ROOMS

2   10.000   2   6.000
COL   COL

"DINING SET"

SAMM HOUSE
OCT. 87!

camden 'set'

TELECOM SLUG

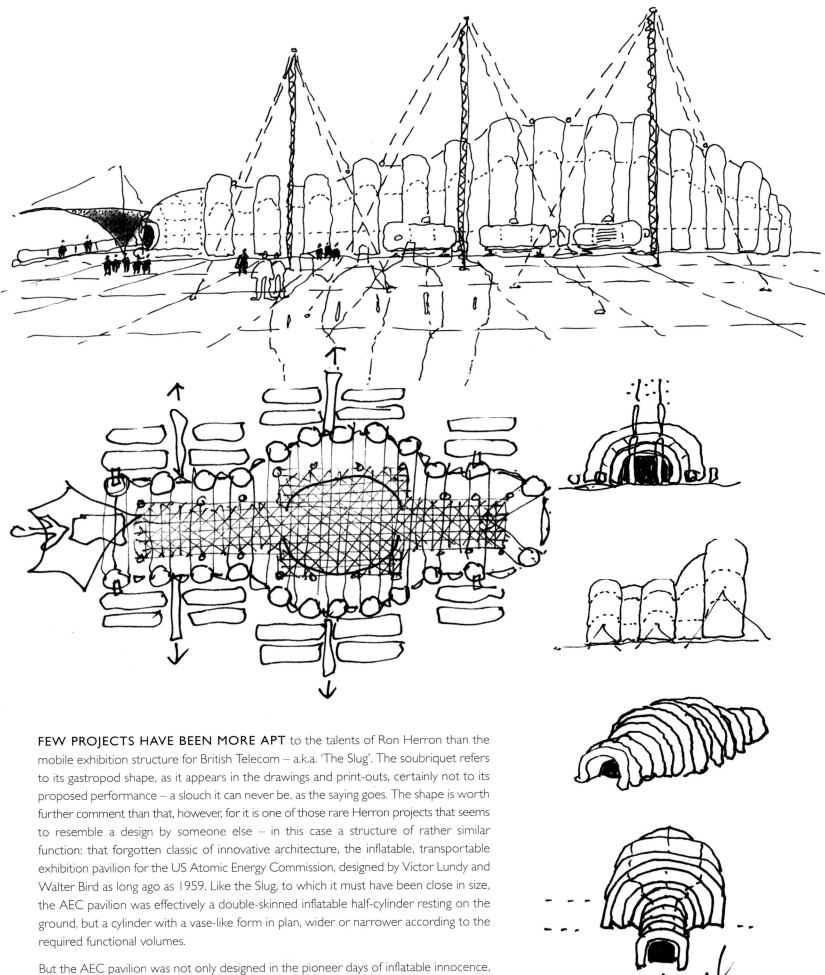

FEW PROJECTS HAVE BEEN MORE APT to the talents of Ron Herron than the mobile exhibition structure for British Telecom – a.k.a. 'The Slug'. The soubriquet refers to its gastropod shape, as it appears in the drawings and print-outs, certainly not to its proposed performance – a slouch it can never be, as the saying goes. The shape is worth further comment than that, however, for it is one of those rare Herron projects that seems to resemble a design by someone else – in this case a structure of rather similar function: that forgotten classic of innovative architecture, the inflatable, transportable exhibition pavilion for the US Atomic Energy Commission, designed by Victor Lundy and Walter Bird as long ago as 1959. Like the Slug, to which it must have been close in size, the AEC pavilion was effectively a double-skinned inflatable half-cylinder resting on the ground, but a cylinder with a vase-like form in plan, wider or narrower according to the required functional volumes.

But the AEC pavilion was not only designed in the pioneer days of inflatable innocence, and took more risks than its designers acknowledged; it was also a child of that older Modern Movement that preferred building profiles to be snug and simple. The Slug is

exhibition structure
NOV. 85.

not; it belongs to a more articulated and expansive era, which fancies clip-ons and accessories, and – though technically excused from many legal restrictions because it will always be a temporary structure wherever it stands – the Slug inhabits a world of different requirements and higher (commercial) expectations, and is intended for heavier usage than the pavilion, and under an all-weather regime, too. Hence it will not be moved as a single unit, but in segments (by helicopter), and when in position it will be loosely braced against collapse from a rank of four latticed lighting-towers flanking it on either side.

And it will stand on a concrete slab, which clearly will not be transportable, but poured *in situ* – so what does 'transportable' mean in this case? But here we have entered the mirror-maze of real-world economics and practical management strategies, which have a way of being far more weird than the airy fantasies dreamed up by even the most visionary architects. It appears to make better economic sense to lay a permanent floor-slab for this impermanent structure, and sell it off when the Slug has moved on to its next exhibition site – it will, after all, be a slab well provided with service pick-ups, structural hold-down points, and other useful goodies. Indeed, at the level where one begins to visualise the logistics of managing and moving such an object as the Slug – the size of a small cathedral, remember – systems-thinking begins to have a curiously solvent effect on established architectural concepts like 'a building'. The Slug may well have to be *two* Slugs, or two-and-some-vulgar-fraction Slugs, if it is to satisfy the programmed requirements of actually having one Slug on site for all of the times per annum that its operational calendar stipulates.

FIX

MOVE

B.T.-'BASE'.

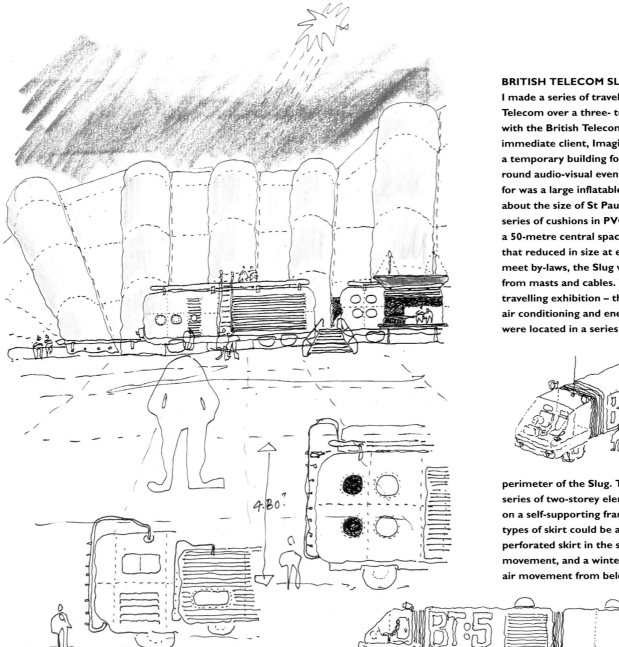

BRITISH TELECOM SLUG

I made a series of travelling exhibitions for British Telecom over a three- to four-year period, starting with the British Telecom Slug in 1985. Our immediate client, Imagination, set the brief to design a temporary building for an exhibition and in-the-round audio-visual event. The version we finally went for was a large inflatable structure with a plan area about the size of St Paul's Cathedral. It consisted of a series of cushions in PVC-coated fabric that spanned a 50-metre central space, forming a half-hemisphere that reduced in size at either end, like a slug. To meet by-laws, the Slug was also externally supported from masts and cables. The service elements of the travelling exhibition – the lavatories, control rooms, air conditioning and energy plants – were located in a series

of 12-metre-long trailers which snuggled up to the perimeter of the Slug. The interior was made up of a series of two-storey elements which were designed on a self-supporting frame and panel system. Two types of skirt could be added around the edge: a perforated skirt in the summer which allowed air movement, and a winter skirt which controlled this air movement from below. As the Slug had to be up and running within three weeks of arriving on site, some advance preparation was necessary. The packages of the inflatable enclosure could be airlifted by helicopter to the site, zipped together, lifted partly on cables, and then inflated, so that the whole erection procedure became part of the show. This was certainly the most ambitious of the BT travelling exhibitions, but there were some objections to what was felt to be a rather comical form. A later version, called **BT City**, used a number of the same elements in a complex, electronically-based exhibition.

And, equally clearly, such a structure, while it may inhabit some segment of real-world economics, does not belong in the normally amortisable world that buildings traditionally inhabit. It is as much the child and servant of the public-relations economy of what we still call Late Capitalism, as are Richard Rogers' Lloyd's Building or Norman Foster's Hongkong and Shanghai Bank. Capitalism aside, however, these monumental comparisons are worth making for another reason also; those commercial monuments are architecture, so is this … just about.

Whether Ron Herron stops any longer to make distinctions between designing buildings, or near-buildings, or kits that periodically add up to quasi-buildings, or whatever, I very much doubt, but every so often he comes up with something like the Slug which seems light-years away from what one commonly considers to be a building – and, dammit! the thing is still architecture.

The shaping of the half-vase envelope itself was done by kneading a straight half-tube in and out on the computer screen, without any further drawings having to be drawn on paper after the first one had been loaded into the machine. But it is still an architectural temperament at work, asking the screen architectural questions and rewarding itself with architectural answers, even – or perhaps even more so – when braced against functional and economic and image demands they never tell you about at architecture school.

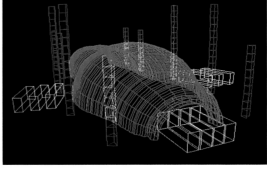

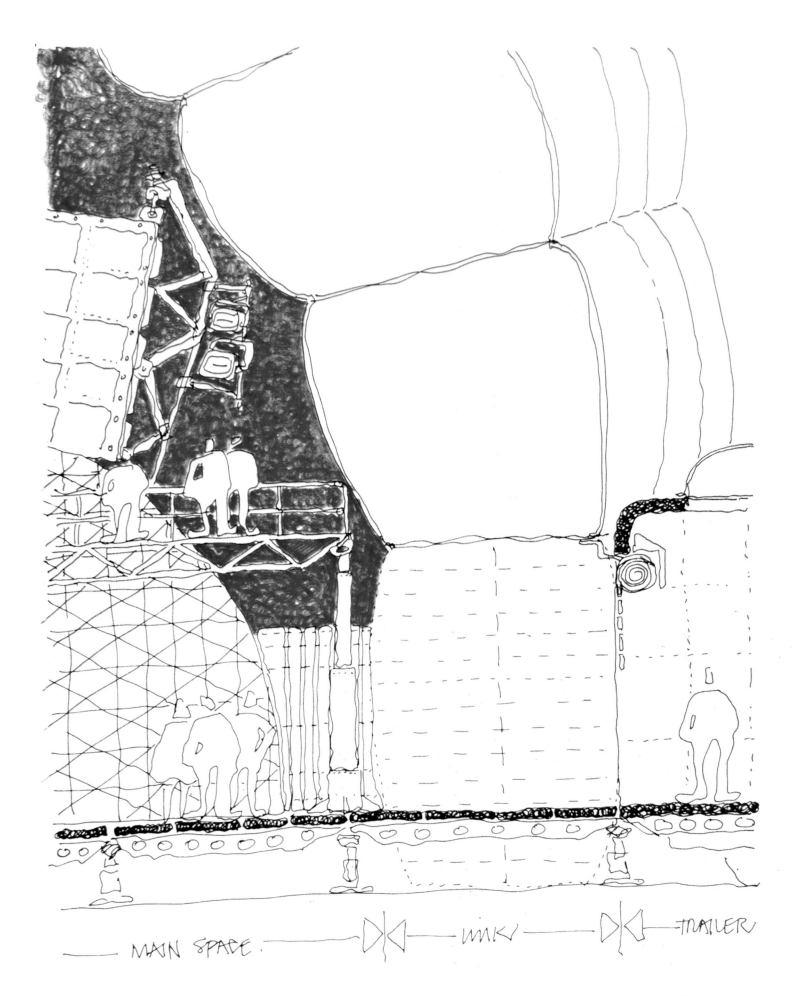

MAIN SPACE — ▷|◁ — LINK — ▷|◁ — TRAILER

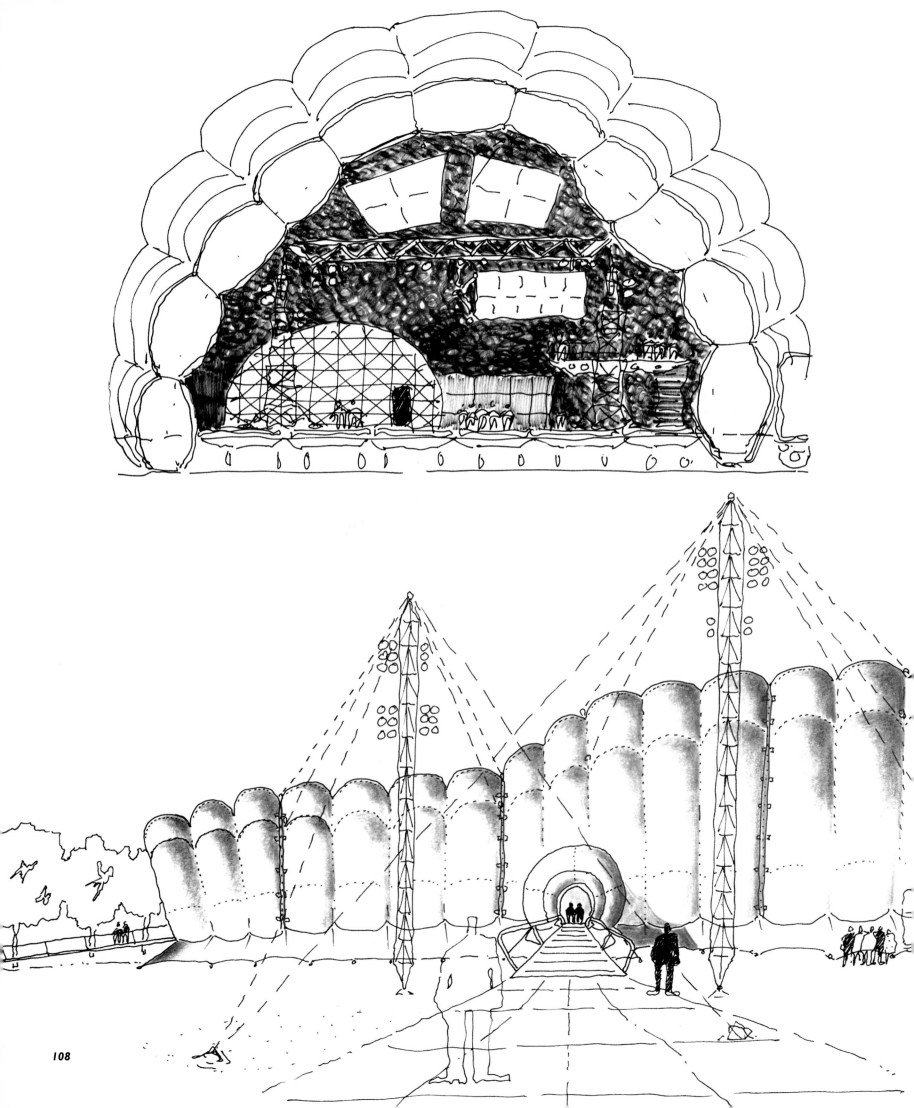

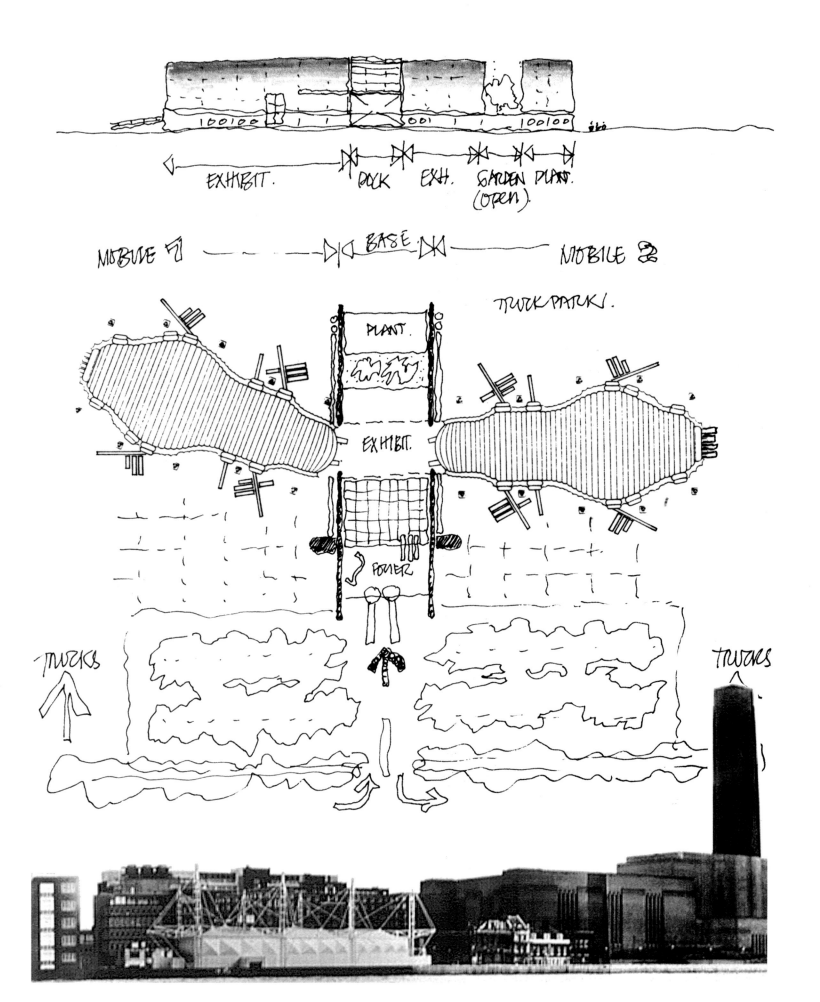

EXHIBIT.   DOCK   EXH.   GARDEN PLANT.
(OPEN)

MOBILE 7 —— —— BASE —— MOBILE 2

TRUCK PARK.

PLANT.

EXHIBIT.

POWER

TRUCKS   TRUCKS

110

Telecoms Aug 85!

'Entrance Gate'

BT City.
24 March 87'.

DIGITAL DESIGN

'RON MAKES A DRAWING FIRST in his notebook in R50 Pentel ballpen and then Andrew puts it into the computer – which is the most labour-intensive part of the whole business.' All computer explanations in the office of Ron Herron Associates have this hands-on quality… and for good reason. The computer image that results must be changeable, rotatable, consultable and all that, but never precious in the way a hard-won hand-drawn axonometric would be. There are certain software limitations on what can be done, even on the most sophisticated hard- and software, which they (unconsciously?) accommodate, but basically they can change the drawing in any particular or detail they like and then see what the side-effects are. In other words, they can monitor the effects of re-design almost instantaneously, and can go on accumulating revisions without sweating blood. More importantly, they can do it without generating labour-intensive works of art that are too hard-won to discard; the basic image in the computer program is always there somewhere in the digital storage, and can be summoned back at the clack of a couple of keys.

This is something different from merely 'mechanising the process', as in conventional offices where the computer is simply used as a kind of clerk for accounts, or as an in-house drafting agency for the production of boring drawings. Children of the Archigram photo-litho revolution, (c.f. their use of 20/80 Xerox to cut and paste imagery) they understand that the mechanism changes the process it mechanises, and exploit it creatively for those reasons… And the end product should be, with luck, a client-friendly video comprehensible to lay eyes, but still accurately reflecting/recording the direct design-activity of the act of *disegno* (i.e., in a way that, say, a model made by a skilled model-maker would not).

An ambition – to cross-link the video/drafting and the production-drawings aspects, so that the results of changes in specification or form can be shown to the client immediately and in detail. Much of this can be done already on heavy duty main-frame computer installations, but to shrink it down to personal-computer dimensions would be to take power – big power – out of the clutches of the corporate establishment and put it back into the hands (literally) of individual architects. The office of Ron Herron is not alone in these ambitions or hands-on experiments, but having one of Britain's best young hackers more or less on tap at any time gives them the competitive edge on other small offices, and being a small office gives them an edge in flexibility over those much larger offices that have built up comparable abilities, institutionally and incrementally, since the late 1950s.

Ultimately, however, the Herron advantage is that they enjoy messing with computers and are not in awe of thinking-machines. And out of this comes the sort of audacity to think in terms of presenting one of their projects as the architectural equivalent of a music-video. The Frankfurt animation was really a very modest enterprise, if measured against the animation industry, but a real-time eye-opener if measured against some architectural animations that have come out of, say, SOM in Chicago, which are heavily touted but found to be the same boring old helicopter tour of Wire-frame City that we have been seeing for twenty years or more.

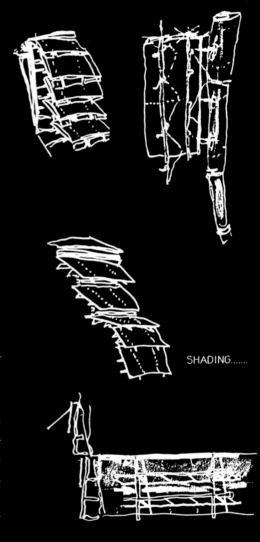

SHADING.......

GLAZING SYSTEM – LAYERING

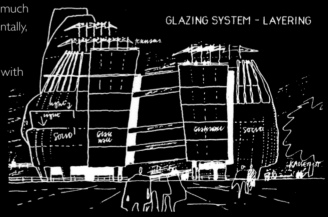

L'ORÉAL

The scheme for the L'Oréal headquarters in Karlsruhe was the result of a limited competition. The brief was quite simple, calling for a building with three quite independent elements: administration, a product and marketing centre, and a hairdressing school. The site was right in the centre of Karlsruhe, in an area that had been almost completely rebuilt after the bombing of the Second World War. The setting was like an encyclopedia of postwar architecture, with everything from functional buildings of the early 1950s to pink Post-Modern buildings of the late 1980s. We felt that the context was so scrambled that it required a strong, powerful building, which could stand in its own right.

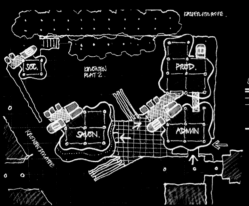

Our solution was a series of three short, stumpy towers, with an additional little tower, the 'children's building', which could be presented to the city as a crèche, or old people's place cum summer theatre. The buildings were set in a dance-like rhythm across the site, visually occupying the space. The forms were deliberately soft where movement occurred, then angular and leaning out over the central space. The project was made at the time when we'd just got the ModelShop software for our Apple Macintosh so, with great excitement, we started on the modelling right away. This is a technique we've used ever since: very early modelling, followed by a gradual refinement right through the design process to create the version that we're happy with at the end of the day.

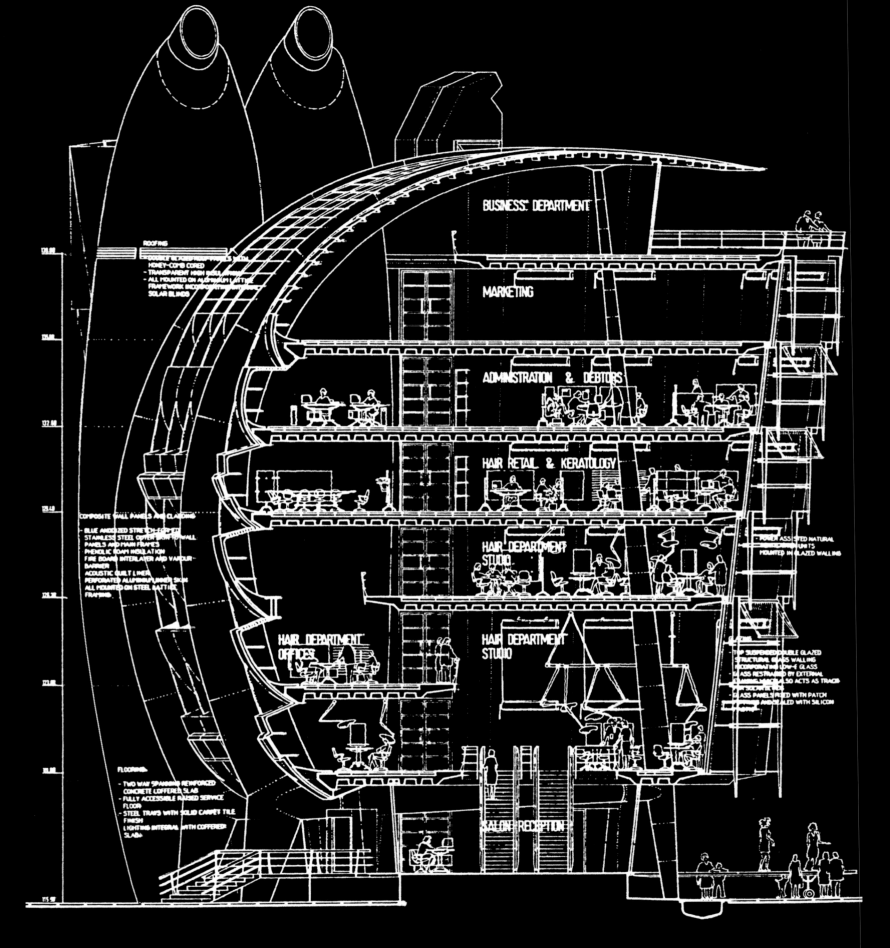

BUSINESS DEPARTMENT

MARKETING

ADMINISTRATION & DEBTORS

HAIR RETAIL & KERATOLOGY

HAIR DEPARTMENT STUDIO

HAIR DEPARTMENT OFFICES

HAIR DEPARTMENT STUDIO

SALON RECEPTION

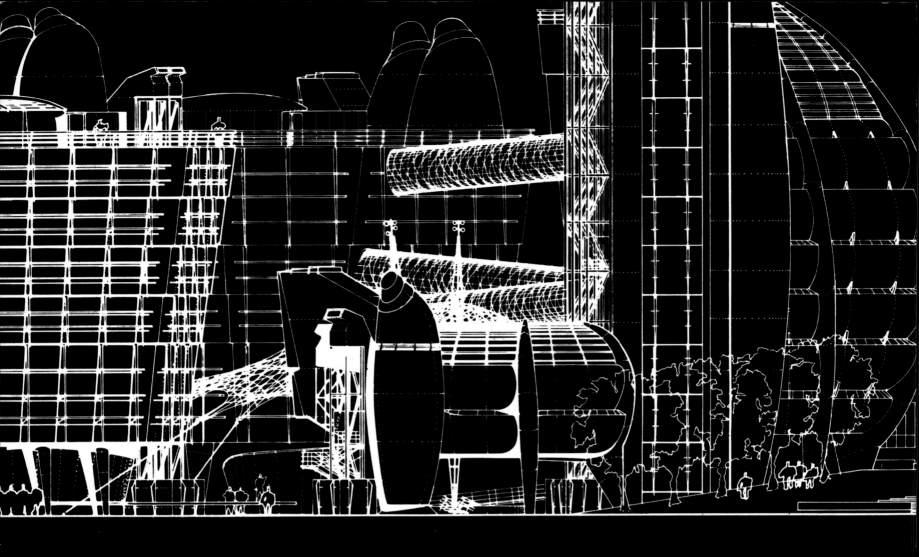

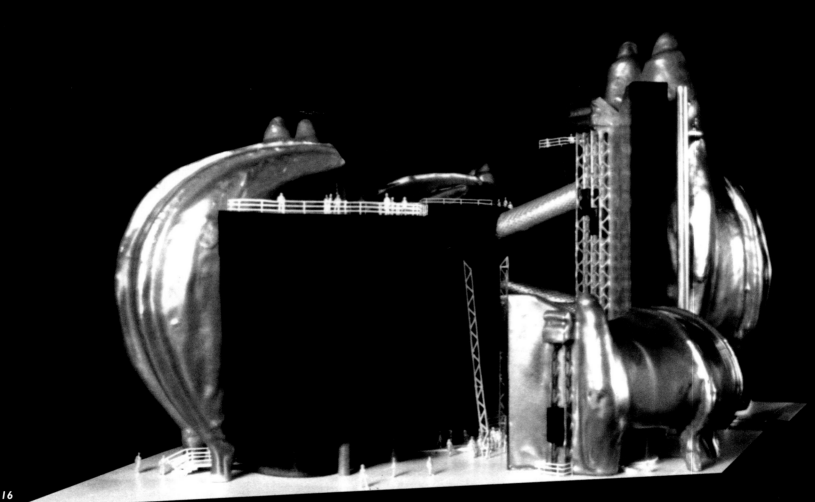

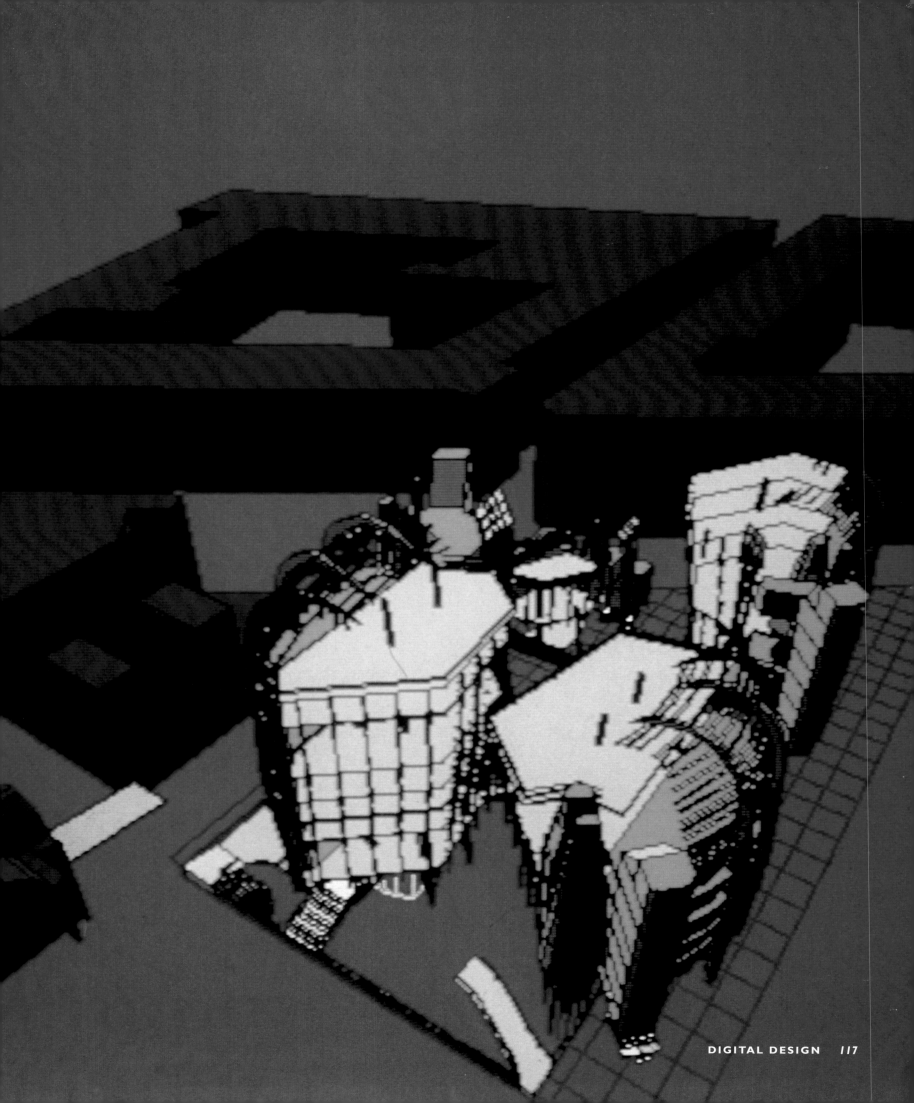

HARBLESIDE

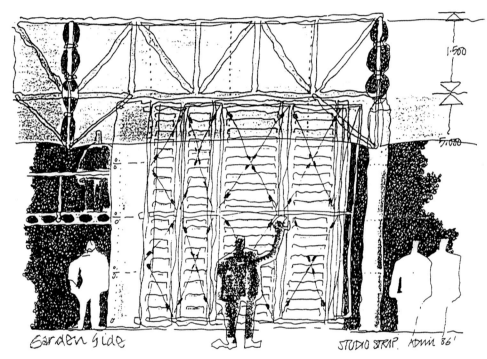

Garden Side

STUDIO STRIP. Admin 86'

1·500

5·000

STUDIO STRIP

Following the Robohouse I made a project called Studio Strip, continuing a fascination with the idea of the robotised building which began, I suppose, with an early Archigram project, Control and Choice, and with the House for the Year 1990 exhibition at Harrods. The idea was to make a strip or terrace of studio dwellings which consisted purely of a roof on a frame. The oddball thing was that the parts that made up the house – the walls, upper floor and screen elements – were entirely robotised so they could be driven into other positions to respond to the user. The screen on the garden side, for example, was a drivable curved video wall, some 15 metres long and 6 metres high, which could be hinged to open outwards. You could therefore see the real garden, or play a video on the wall of any environment that you wished to be in, or even drive the wall right out into the garden, taking the idea of indoor/outdoor architecture to an extreme. The design was also of interest because it allowed us to experiment with one of our early computer models, after we managed to convince an animation studio to animate it for us. With Dennis Crompton, who did some trickery with the backcloths, we made a video that was eventually shown at the German Architecture Museum in the 1986 exhibition, *VISION DER MODERNE*. The video starts with an animated walk into the Studio Strip. Then you see me sitting in the computer model with moving images on the video wall behind me – I'm in a real space talking about real images. In the end sequence the screen opens, and I'm sitting in my own garden finishing the conversation.

This animation sequence was an early attempt of ours to simulate a real environment, I still find it quite fascinating.

The Frankfurt number is about the then latest instalments in the Suburban Sets saga, but it is also about architecture-video, building up from empty wire-frame to solid architecture complete with shadows, as well as doing the usual rotations and perspective-cruise routines. It is also about Ron Herron himself, talking in/about/in front of the solid facades of some real world suburbia, and then inside the video simulation of the Strip House, and finally in his own backyard as revealed by rolling back the rear wall of the simulation. It's all jolly Post-Modern, not in the routine 'Look-Mum-I-can-do-Palladian-Windows' architectural manner, but in the 'Modes-of-Discourse-about-Discourse' manner that has lately engaged the minds of heavier-than-architectural thinkers in academe. Like a Post-Modern novelist abandoning the Almighty Author stance of traditional writers in favour of the more modest Untrustworthy Narrator posture of the writer who is part of his own fiction, Ron Herron presents himself in the video as part of his own design project, far more convincingly than does, say, James Stirling in the famous perspectives of his own Olivetti Milton Keynes project.

For, where the draftsmanly convention of Rob Krier's drawings of-and-for Stirling cannot but present Big Jim as the Almighty Architect of tradition, Ron Herron, speaking *in propria voce* from the overgrown private garden behind his own

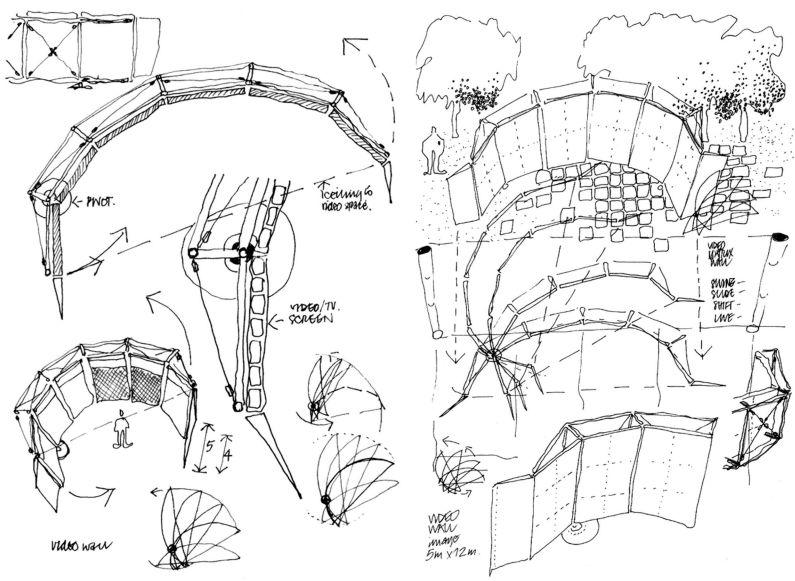

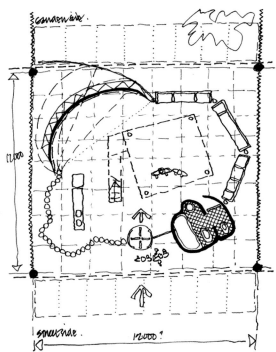

computer simulation, presents himself as a user-friendly illusion just like you or me (only without making a big deal out of it, like some novelist hung up on 'narratology'). The architect who has always been metaphorically at home *with* technology, here – thanks to his personal computer – appears as a mean-sensual man who is literally at home in technology. And, perhaps, in that flourishing backyard that is real despite the graphic illusions of robot domesticity by which we have come at it, he can begin to discern for us that elusive essence of technology that technologists cannot elucidate – without ever ceasing to be the architect he has always been.

But now the constant presence of the architectural temperament has to be measured against a shifting panoply of ever-cleverer software, whose taxonomy and naming have little to do with the ancient vocabularies of *disegno*. Although the information about to be offered may be as dead as the pharaohs of Egypt by the time these words are *published*, at the time these words are *written* the office has been using MacDraft with MiniCad as an effective design tool, and also experimenting with Glue as a means of extracting material from Schema so that it can be worked on with MacDraft or whatever. The software names will mostly fade from importance, the endeavour that bends them to the architectural will can never fade, however – not while architecture persists, not while architects like Ron Herron persist in making architecture.

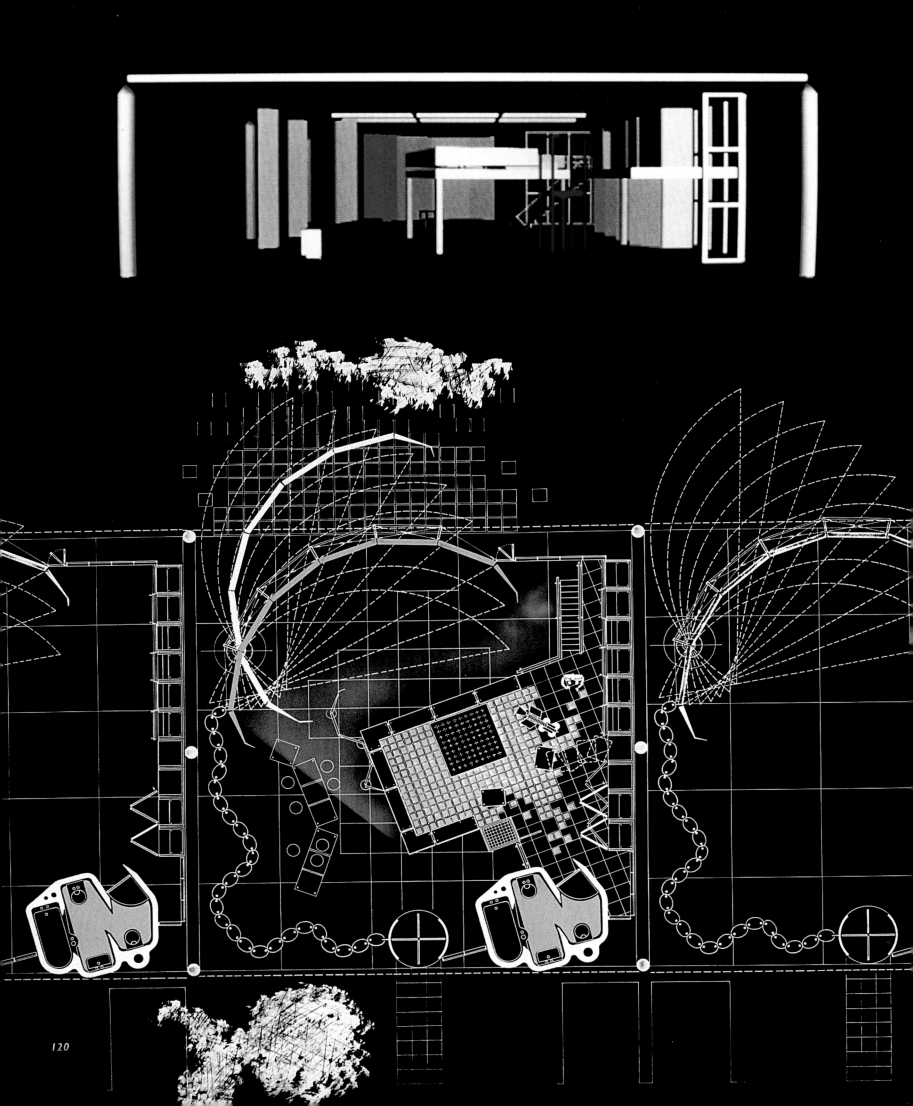

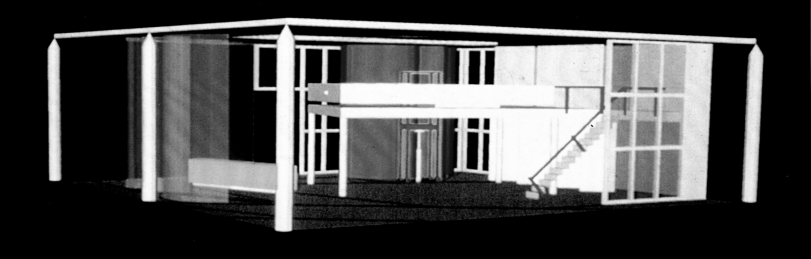

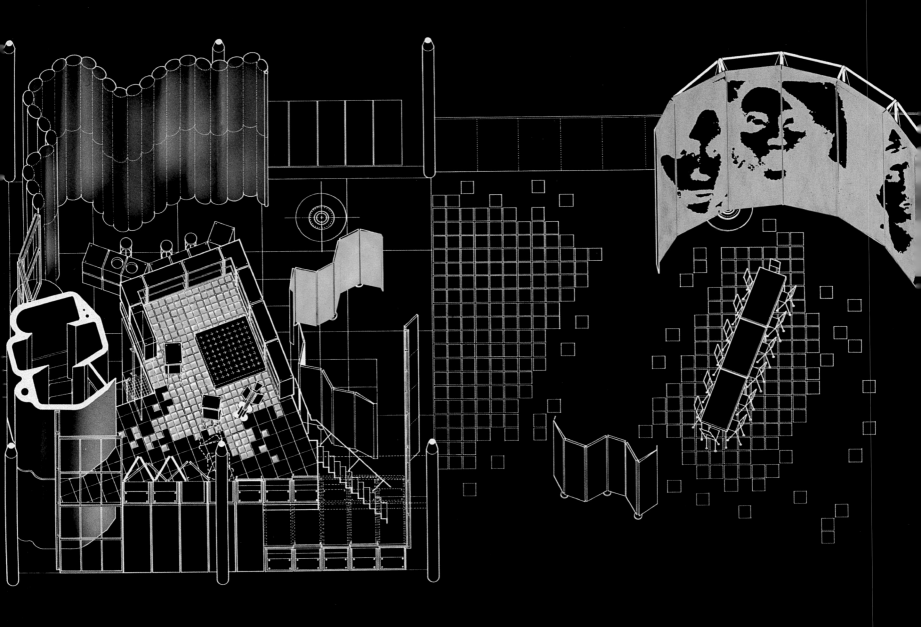

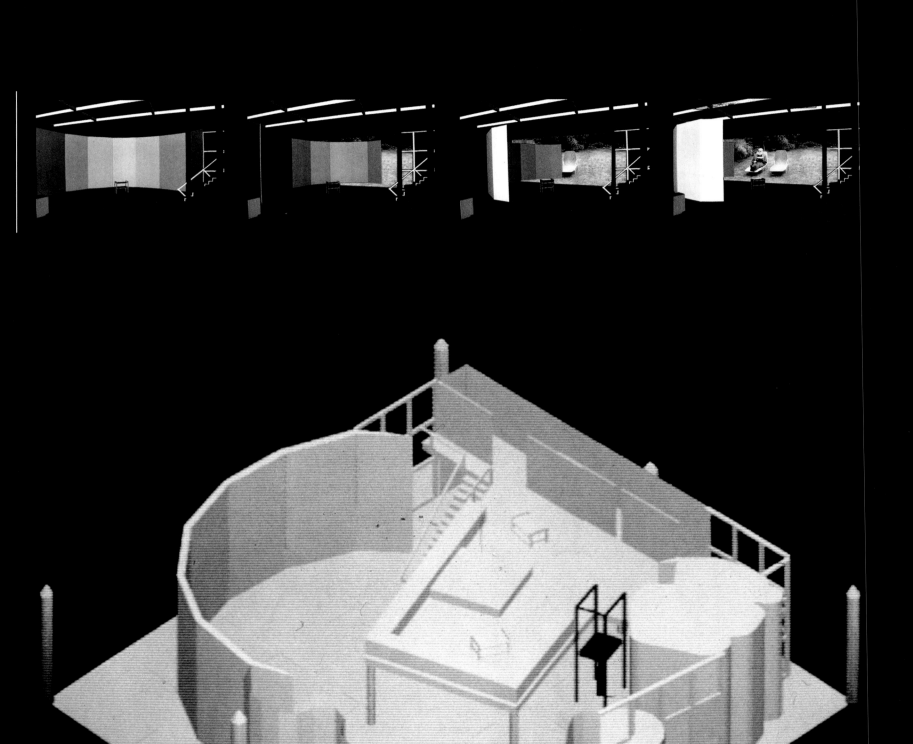

RON HERRON
ARIBA FCSD FRSA

A Londoner who, aged 15, went to the Brixton School of Building to learn carpentry, but discovered architecture • First job, in a one-man architectural practice, was as assistant/typist/telephonist/teamaker • Studied architecture at evening school, firstly at Brixton and later at the Polytechnic, Regent Street • In 1952 married Pat, his girlfriend from the age of 16 • Son, Andrew, born in 1958 • After completing National Service in the RAF (Ron is a 'veteran' of the Berlin airlift) joined London County Council Architects' Department in 1954 and met Warren Chalk and Dennis Crompton, and, through a mutual friend, Peter Cook, David Greene and Mike Webb • In 1962 they together joined the Euston Project team with Robin Middleton, Brian Richards, Frank Linden and Alex Pike under Theo Crosby • The Archigram Group was born in this period and combined to produce *Archigram* magazine • Son, Simon, born in 1963 • Commenced teaching at the Architectural Association in 1965 and continued, apart from a two-year gap, until 1993 • Joined Warren Chalk in 1968 as Visiting Professor at the University of California Los Angeles • Like Reyner Banham, fell in love with Los Angeles • Lived there for two years, and has managed a visit each year since • Returned in 1970 to form the Archigram office, with Peter Cook and Dennis Crompton, on winning the Monte Carlo competition; after three years the project was shelved and the Archigram office closed in 1975 • Joined Pentagram and became a partner 1977-81 • Formed Herron Associates in 1982; joined by his sons, Andrew (1985) and Simon (1988) • Merged with Imagination Ltd, after completion of its headquarters in Store Street, London, as Herron Associates at Imagination in 1989 • Re-established Herron Associates as an independent architectural practice with son Andrew and became Professor and Head of the School of Architecture at the University of East London (UEL) during 1993 • A Leo, an optimist, enjoys the company of his friends; quiet, an Arsenal fan, draws to illustrate his ideas rather than writing about them, and believes that 'any sufficiently advanced technology is magic.'

PROFESSIONAL CAREER

1954-61 Architect with the London County Council/Greater London Council
1960 Founder member, with Warren Chalk, Peter Cook, Dennis Crompton, Mike Webb and David Greene, Archigram Group, London
1960-70 Co-Editor of *Archigram* Magazine
1961-65 Deputy Architect, Taylor Woodrow Construction Ltd, London
1965-67 Associate, Halpern & Partners, London
1967 Consultant Architect to Colin St John Wilson, Cambridge
1968 In private practice, London
1969-70 Director of Urban Design, William L Pereira Associates, Los Angeles
1970-75 Partner with Cook and Crompton, Archigram Architects, London
1975-77 Private practice, London
1977-81 Partner, Pentagram Design, London
1981-82 Derek Walker Associates, Milton Keynes & London
1982-84 Principal, Ron Herron Associates, London
1984-89 Partner, Herron Associates, London
1989-93 Director, Imagination Ltd (Herron Assocs merges with Imagination)
1993- Partner, Herron Associates, London

TEACHING

1965-93 Tutor, Architectural Association School, London
1968 North London Polytechnic School of Architecture
1968-69 Visiting Professor, UCLA, Los Angeles
1972 Artist-in-Residence, University of Wisconsin, Madison
1976, 1977,1979,1991 University of Southern California, Los Angeles
1982 Southern California Institute for Architecture, Los Angeles
1992-93 Visiting Professor, The Bartlett School of Architecture, London
1993- Professor and Head of School of Architecture, University of East London

PROJECTS

1954-57
Prospect County Secondary School, St Pancras, London (LCC)
1957
Paisley Technical College Competition (with Warren Chalk), Second Prize
1958
Enfield Civic Centre Competition (with Warren Chalk)
Student Hostel, Northampton College of Advanced Tech., London (LCC)
Hotel Study, South Bank, London (with Alan Forrest) (LCC)
Television Centre, South Bank, London (with Alan Forrest) (LCC)
1958-61
Woolwich Polytechnic Extension, London (LCC)
1959
Halesowen Housing Competition (with Warren Chalk), Second Prize
Sunday Times National Gallery Competition (with Warren Chalk)
BEA Office and Terminal, Manchester (with Warren Chalk)
1960
BEA Office, Regent Street, London (with Warren Chalk)
BEA Office Carlton Street, London (with Warren Chalk)
1961
BEA Terminal, Guernsey (with Warren Chalk)
Lincoln Civic Centre Comp. (with Warren Chalk and Dennis Crompton)
Lillington Street Housing Comp. (with Warren Chalk and Dennis Crompton)
1961-63
South Bank Development (Queen Elizabeth Hall and Hayward Gallery) (with Warren Chalk and Dennis Crompton) (LCC)
1962
Liverpool University Halls of Residence Competition (with Warren Chalk)
1962-65
Euston Station Redevelopment, London (with Theo Crosby)
1963
City Interchange Project (with Warren Chalk)
Living City Exhibition, ICA, London (with Archigram Group)
1964
Study of Twilight Areas: Fulham (with Theo Crosby)
'Walking City' Project.
Ulster Museum Competition (with Bryan Harvey), Second Prize
Stand for IBSAC Exhibition, Project
1965
HQ for Clarkson Shipping, London (with Theo Crosby)
Gasket Homes Project (with Warren Chalk)
Capsule Pier Project
Industrialised Hospital Building, Reading (with Dennis Crompton)
Monorail Transportation Study and Exhibition (with Dennis Crompton)

Leisure Zone Project – Seaside Net

Airhouse Project, Cardiff Castle Exhibition

Industrialised Housing Project, Southall, London (with Dennis Crompton and Peter Cook)

1966

FreeTime Inflatable Dwelling Project (with Barry Snowden)

Leisure Study: Inflatable Units for Land, Sea and Air

1967

Free Time Node Trailer Cage

Air Hab and Air Hab Village (with Barry Snowden)

FreeTime Node (with Barry Snowden)

Living 1990: Project and Exhibition, Harrods, London (with Archigram Group)

Control & Choice: Housing Study and Exhibit at the Paris Biennale (with Dennis Crompton and Peter Cook)

St Katherine's Dock Development (with Dennis Crompton and Peter Cook)

1968

Archigram Exhibit at the Fourteenth Milan Triennale (with Archigram Group)

Tuned Suburbs Project

Oasis Project

Instant City Project: Funded by the Graham Foundation, Chicago (with Dennis Crompton and Peter Cook)

Instant City at Los Angeles

Urban Action Tune-Up

Instant City in the Desert

Holographis Scene-Setter

Self-Destruct Environ-Pole

Housing Development, Santa Monica, California (with Warren Chalk)

1969

Manzak Robot Project

Enviro-Pill Project

Long Beach Entertainment Park, California

Kassel Documenta Eventstructure (with Peter Cook)

Design of Master Plan for a New Town for the Ford Motor Company at Dearborn, Michigan (with William L Pereira Associates)

1969-73

'Features Monte Carlo', Entertainment Facility, Winning Design, Invited International Competition (with Archigram)

1970

Design of Air Terminal at Los Angeles International Airport for Pan American Airlines (with William L Pereira Associates)

Project for Hotel and Offices for Ford on the Embarcadero Site, San Francisco (with William L Pereira Associates)

Project for Teaching Facility for the University of Missouri (with William L Pereira Associates)

Archigram Capsule at Expo '70, Osaka, Japan (with Archigram Group)

Instant City Airship Project

Bournemouth Steps Project (with Dennis Crompton and Peter Cook)

British Rail and British Industry Exhibits at the Louvre, Paris, for the COI (with Dennis Crompton and Peter Cook)

1971

'Palm Tree' Project for Monte Carlo Summer Casino (with Dennis Crompton)

1972

Promotional Event Kit (with Barry Snowden)

Development Plan for Margate, Kent (with Dennis Crompton)

'It's A…' Project

Tuning London Project (with Diana Jowsey)

1973

Swimming Pool and Kitchen Block for Rod Stewart, Windsor, Berkshire (with Dennis Crompton)

Northampton Civic Centre Competition (with Archie McNab)

Glasgow Riverfront Competition (with Archie McNab)

Offices for BOC, Dublin (with Dennis Crompton)

1974

Malaysia Exhibition, Commonwealth Inst. London. (with Dennis Crompton)

Furniture for Cassina, Milan (with Peter Cook)

'Suburban Sets' Project (with Andrew Herron)

Student Centre Competition, Trondheim, Norway (with Cedric Price, Per Kartvedt, Tony Dugdale, Dennis Crompton and Peter Cook)

1975

Play Centre at Calverton End, Milton Keynes (with Dennis Crompton)

'Sets Fit for the Queen' Project

Theatre Extension Proposal, Trondheim, Norway (with Per Kartvedt)

Outdoor Exhibition Space, Commonwealth Institute, London (with Dennis Crompton)

1976

Design for the Development of the Central Area of Heathrow Airport, London (with Dennis Crompton and Wolff Olins)

Government Offices Competition, Vienna (with Theo Crosby)

1977

St Christopher's Place Development, London (with Pentagram)

Trondheim Library Competition, Norway

1978

Bubble Theatre Company, Inflatable Theatre Project (with Pentagram)

Offices for Chrysalis Records, London (with Pentagram)

Offices for A.T. Kearney, Piccadilly, London (with Pentagram)

Cape Products Exhibit, Building Exhibition, Birmingham (with Pentagram)

1979

Directors Studio, Offices & Studio, London (with Pentagram)

Boston Consultancy Group Offices, London (with Pentagram)

New Confravision Studio and Business Centre for British Telecom, Bristol, Avon (with Pentagram)

Public Library Competition, Stavanger, Norway

1980

DOM Office Headquarters, Cologne, Germany, Competition (with Peter Cook and Christine Hawley)

Stromberger Factory Site Development, Clichy, Paris (with Pentagram)

Pentagram Exhibit, Linz, Austria (with Alan Fletcher)

Reuters Office, Press Centre, London (with Pentagram)

Swan & Edgar Department Store Development, London (with Pentagram)

Congress Hall Berlin Competition – 'Soft Collapse'

Eames House Remodelled – Ideas Competition

1981

Jubail City Business Centre Plan (with Derek Walker Associates)

Urban Sets Competition Project (with Andrew and Simon Herron)

Design of Wonderworld Theme Park, Corby, Northamptonshire (with Derek Walker)

1982 Formed Ron Herron Associates

London Offices and Hairdressing School for L'Oréal Golden Limited (with Walker Wright)

Blackrod Video Production Studio and Offices, London

Lyric Theatre Demountable Rehearsal Space, Hammersmith, London

Bankside Power Station Entertainment Complex, Conversion Study